Aveline Kushi's Wonderful World of Salads

Aveline Kushi's Wonderful World of Salads

Aveline Kushi
and Wendy Esko

Japan Publications, Inc.

Note to the reader: It is advisable to seek the guidance of a qualified health professional and macrobiotic counselor before implementing the dietary and other suggestions for specific conditions presented in this book. It is essential that any reader who has any reason to suspect serious illness in themselves or their family members seek appropriate advice promptly. Neither this or any other book should be used as a substitute for qualified care or treatment.

Published by JAPAN PUBLICATIONS, INC., Tokyo and New York

Distributors:
UNITED STATES: *Kodansha International/USA, Ltd., 114 Fifth Avenue, New York, N. Y. 10011.* CANADA: *Fitzhenry & Whiteside Ltd., 195 Allstate Parkway, Markham, Ontario, L3R 4T8.* MEXICO AND CENTRAL AMERICA: *HARLA S. A. de C. V., Apartado 30–546, Mexico 4, D. F.* BRITISH ISLES: *Premier Book Marketing Ltd., 1 Gower Street, London WC1E 6HA.* EUROPEAN CONTINENT: *European Book Service PBD, Strijkviertel 63, 3454 PK De Meern, The Netherlands.* AUSTRALIA AND NEW ZEALAND: *Bookwise International, 54 Crittenden Road, Findon, South Australia 5007.* THE FAR EAST AND JAPAN: *Japan Publications Trading Co., Ltd., 1–2–1, Sarugaku-cho, Chiyoda-ku, Tokyo 101.*

First edition: May 1989

LCCC No. 88–81759
ISBN 0–87040–785–6

Printed in U.S.A.

Foreword

Throughout the world, salads symbolize freshness and lightness in meals. They make us think of warm summer days and quick, light, and refreshing dishes. Salads increase our awareness and appreciation of the endless variety of foods in the vegetable kingdom.

To the macrobiotic cook, salads are far more than simple servings of lettuce. Macrobiotics is a way of living and eating in harmony with the environment. It is based on the flexible adaptation of universal principles to life's changing circumstances. The range of foods and cooking methods used in macrobiotics is as broad and diverse as nature itself.

This book is not simply a collection of delicious and healthful salad recipes. It is a guidebook to achieving health and well-being through a way of eating and living in harmony with nature. Practical suggestions are presented for changing from a modern high-fat, high-cholesterol diet toward a diet high in complex carbohydrates and fiber. We detail numerous ways to include salads as a part of this wholesome way of eating.

Our discussion of diet begins with the principles of macrobiotics, including how to balance yin and yang energies in food and why this is important for health and well-being. These principles of balance and harmony can help everyone create a healthful diet under any circumstances. We then describe the standard macrobiotic diet, which is based on the dynamic balance between yin and yang, and show how a variety of salad dishes can be incorporated as a part of this balanced dietary pattern.

Also presented are suggestions for a healthful lifestyle that complement the practice of the macrobiotic diet. We conclude the introductory section with a discussion of cooking itself, and explain how different methods of cooking can be used to rebalance the energy in food to meet individual needs and preferences.

The recipe chapters begin with step-by-step instructions for preparing a wide variety of garnishes, dressings, and condiments that add flavor, nutrition, and elegance to salads. The salads themselves are arranged according to the type of food used as the main ingredient, and generally follow the order of the standard macrobiotic diet. Included are recipes for a variety of delicious and healthful whole-grain, noodle, and pasta salads, vegetable, bean, tofu, and sea vegetable salads, and light fruit salads and kantens.

Recipes for specialty dishes, such as home-made sushi, pickles, and pressed and boiled salads are also presented. Preparing these dishes can help you become familiar with an incredibly wide range of whole natural foods and cooking methods. We recommend using only all-natural ingredients, without sugar, saturated fats, or refined table salt. These salads are rich in complex carbohydrates, vitamins, and fiber. They add nutrition and taste to any meal.

We would like to thank everyone who contributed to this book. We thank

Michio Kushi for furthering the understanding of food and its relationship to human health and well-being through his lectures, writing, and personal guidance. We also thank Edward Esko for help in writing the introductory chapters, and for guidance with the book as a whole. We thank Cindy Briscoe, a teacher of macrobiotic cooking in Kansas City, for the wonderful illustrations of garnishes and cutting methods, and thank Mariko Fry, who with the help of her husband Chris, did the lovely brush style drawings of salad dishes and utensils in the recipe chapters and glossary. We also thank the Japan Publications staff in Tokyo for their proofreading and editorial work, and express appreciation to Mr. Iwao Yoshizaki and Mr. Yoshiro Fujiwara, respectively president and New York representative of Japan Publications, Inc., for their ongoing encouragement and support.

Aveline Kushi
Wendy Esko
Becket, Massachusetts
January, 1989

Contents

Foreword, 5

Chapter 1: The Energy of Food, 9

Chapter 2: Macrobiotic Eating, 19

Chapter 3: The Yin and Yang of Salad, 31

Chapter 4: The Art of Garnishing, 45

Chapter 5: Condiments, Dressings, and Dips, 88

Chapter 6: Whole Grain and Pasta Salads, 105

Chapter 7: Fresh Vegetable Salads, 118

Chapter 8: Bean and Tofu Salads, 135

Chapter 9: Sea-vegetable Salads, 144

Chapter 10: Fruit Salads and Kanten, 151

Glossary of Utensils, 159
Macrobiotic Resources, 163
Recommended Reading, 165
About the Authors, 169
Index, 171

Chapter 1

The Energy of Food

Today, people everywhere are seeking a lighter, healthier diet. They are moving away from fatty, cholesterol-rich foods toward low-fat cuisine. They are eating more whole grains and fewer refined foods, increasing their intake of complex carbohydrates, and reducing their consumption of simple sugars. And they are using more fresh vegetables and fruits and fewer canned and frozen foods. These and other positive dietary changes are often motivated by a desire for better health. As an example of how widespread dietary awareness has become in the last decade, about eight million Americans now call themselves vegetarians, according to *Time* magazine (March 7, 1988). Many new vegetarians have shifted away from animal products and toward natural, vegetable-quality foods in the last five years.

The popularity of salad is an example of the growing movement toward balanced nutrition. Over the past ten years, salad bars have appeared in restaurants across the country, and for many people, dining out now means ordering low-fat seafood and salad. Moreover, numerous schools and colleges now feature salad bars, and report that they are very popular with students.

Salads are quick and easy to make. When prepared with fresh natural ingredients and served in balanced proportions, they can be an important part of a healthier diet. They add vitamins, minerals, enzymes, and fiber to the diet, and a fresh, light touch to meals.

Preparing healthful and delicious salads can challenge the imagination and creativity of both beginning and experienced cooks. Salads can be made with an incredible variety of natural ingredients—from whole grain pasta to sea vegetables, and from *kasha* to bean sprouts. In preparing natural salad dressings, a cook can also become familiar with a wide range of whole natural foods.

In the chapters that follow, we describe the art of making healthful and appetizing salads, and how to include them in a naturally balanced diet. We also present recipes for natural salad dressings, quick, light pickles, pressed salads, and garnishes.

The approach to food and cooking that we present in this book is known throughout the world today as "macrobiotics." The word comes from the Greek *macro*, meaning "large" or "great," and *bios*, meaning "life." It describes a way of living and eating in harmony with nature, for the purpose of achieving health, happiness, and peace.

For over thirty years, macrobiotic education has been at the forefront of the growing nutritional awareness in America, Europe, and other parts of the world. In the 1960s, our macrobiotic friends in Boston helped launch the natural food movement. Today, as the result of these efforts, millions of people use whole grains, fresh local vegetables, *tofu, miso, tamari* soy sauce, sea vegetables, and other whole, natural foods on a daily basis. Many people have experienced improvement in their health and well-being as a result of adopting the macrobiotic diet, including recovery from serious illness.

Moreover, during the past decade, leading public health agencies have issued dietary guidelines that parallel macrobiotics. The preventive dietary guidelines of the U.S. Senate Select Committee on Nutrition and Human Needs, the American Heart Association, the National Academy of Sciences, and the American Cancer Society are similar in orientation to the macrobiotic diet. In this book, you will learn how to apply guidelines such as these in the kitchen, while preparing a variety of nutritious and appetizing dishes. As you will discover in these pages, healthful eating can be delicious and fun.

Food is a vital link to the world around us. The foods we select and the way in which we cook and eat them enable us to balance the changing environment and our personal needs. The principle of balance, known in macrobiotics as *yin* and *yang*, is simple yet comprehensive. It can be invaluable in learning how to select the best foods for our particular circumstance. Before we learn about making healthful and delicious salads, let us see how yin and yang can help guide us in selecting the most healthful foods.

Discovering Yin and Yang

One of the best ways to learn about yin and yang is to see how they appear in our daily foods. "Yin" and "yang" are simply terms that we use to represent the most primary forces in nature. Yin represents the primary energy of expansion, and yang, the energy of contraction. These invisible forces create everything in the universe, and manifest on earth as a downward, contracting force that spirals in from the infinite reaches of space (more yang); and an upward, expanding force generated by the earth's rotation (more yin). All motion on the earth, including that of the earth itself, is created by these dynamic forces. They appear everywhere and in everything.

Simply looking at the foods we eat can help us discover how these energies influence them. Although any foods will do, we can begin by observing the shape, size, and other features of several carrots, preferably with the greens attached, a length of burdock root (available at most natural grocers), a hard fall squash, a head of green cabbage, a bunch of mustard greens, and a handful of short-grain brown rice. We recommend that you observe actual foods in order to see how these energies appear.

Begin by placing a carrot on your table or cutting board. Compare the upper part with the tip. Which part has stronger contracting energy? As we can see, the upper portion is wider and more expanded, and the tip narrower and more contracted. Downward or contracting energy is stronger in the tip of the carrot, which is the part that grows deeper in the ground, while upward, or expanding energy is stronger in the upper part.

If the carrot greens are still attached, notice how they grow in a direction that is opposite to the root. The root grows in a downward direction and is more dense or solid than the more delicate stems and leaves that branch upward. These sections complement and make balance with one another.

Looking more closely at the greens, notice how the stems are tighter and more contracted, while the leaves are larger and more expanded. Although the greens are on the whole more expanded than the root, within their structure, certain regions have more expanding, and others, more contracting energy.

Place another carrot on the table. Notice how each vegetable has a different shape and size. One will be longer, the other shorter; one thicker, the other thinner; one straighter, and the other more curved or irregularly shaped. Place one of the carrots in your left hand, and the other in your right. You may notice that one is slightly heavier than the other. Here we see that although they are generally alike, no two carrots have exactly the same proportion of expanding and contracting energies. Each is totally unique.

Now place the burdock root alongside the carrots. Notice how it has a tougher and more fibrous skin. Moreover, burdock root normally grows deeper into the soil than carrots do. If you slice each vegetable in half, you will notice that the burdock is drier and less juicy inside. These qualities indicate that when compared to carrots, burdock root has stronger contracting energy.

Next, place the cabbage and squash on the table with the root vegetables. Think about how these vegetables grow. Burdock and carrots grow further down into the soil, under the influence of strong contracting energy. Round-shaped vegetables grow nearer the surface or above it. In this position, contracting energy is less strong. However, the expanding energy in round-shaped vegetables is not as strong as that in the carrot greens, which grow in a more upward direction. The more rounded shape of these vegetables means that neither upward or downward force is overly predominant. Both are somewhat balanced. From these considerations, we can see that cabbage and squash are more expanded than root vegetables, and more contracted than leafy greens.

Take the mustard greens and place them on the table with the other vegetables. First, compare their size, shape, and structure to the carrot greens. Notice how the carrot tops have a more minute leaf structure. Each leaf is tiny in comparison to the broader mustard leaves. Smaller, more finely differentiated leaves have more contracting energy than broader, more expanded ones. On the whole, leafy greens are more expanded than root or round-shaped vegetables, but among them, some varieties have more expanding and others more contracting energy.

Now place a handful of brown rice on the table. Notice how the grains are harder and more compact than the vegetables, and how they are drier and less juicy. On the whole, brown rice and other cereal grains have more contracting energy than most vegetables. However, even in a handful of rice, each grain will have a different balance of energy. Some will be larger, and others smaller. Most have a ripe golden color (more yang), while a few unripe grains have a green color (more yin). Also, when you wash rice, the more dense or compact grains immediately sink to the bottom, while more expanded ones take longer.

Classifying Food Energies

From these basic examples, we can now begin to judge the qualities of energy in other foods. Aside from things that are readily apparent, such as the size, shape, moisture content, and density of a particular vegetable, a number of other factors are also important. For example, where and in what season the food was grown, its chemical composition, especially the proportion of contracting minerals to more expanding ones, the speed at which it grows, and whether it was grown naturally or with artificial fertilizers and chemicals all play a role in ascertaining the quality of the food.

The factors that help in determining the degree of yinness or yangness in foods can be summarized as follows:

Yin Energy Creates	*Yang Energy Creates*
Growth in a hot climate	Growth in a cold climate
More rapid growth	Slower growth
Foods containing more water	Drier foods
Fruits and leaves, which are more nurtured by expanding energies	Stems, roots, and seeds which are more nurtured by contracting energies
Growth upward high above the ground	Growth downward below the ground
Sour, bitter, sharply sweet, hot, and aromatic foods	Salty, plainly sweet, and pungent foods

When classifying foods, we need to see which of these factors predominates, since as we saw above, all foods have both expanding and contracting energies.

One of the most accurate methods of classification is to observe how the cycle of the seasons influences the growth of the particular plant. During the winter, the climate is colder. At this time of year, energy in the atmosphere becomes more contracting. In plants, leaves wither and die as the sap descends to the roots and the vitality of the plant becomes more condensed. As the earth becomes hard and frozen, branches of trees and other plants become bare, and the grass dries up and turns yellow or brown. Plants used for food and grown in late autumn and winter are drier and more concentrated. They can be kept for a longer time without spoiling. Examples of these plants are carrots, turnips, and cabbages.

During the spring and early summer nature erupts with new life. As the weather becomes hotter, the energy in plants and in the atmosphere ascends and green replaces brown as the predominant color in the vegetable world. Spring and summer plants are more yin in nature. They are more watery and perish more quickly, and provide a cooling effect, which is needed in warm months. In late summer, the energy in plants reaches its zenith as many fruits become ripe. They are very watery and sweet and develop higher above the ground.

The yearly cycle shows how the energies of expansion and contraction alternate

General Yin (▽) and Yang (△) Categorization of Foods

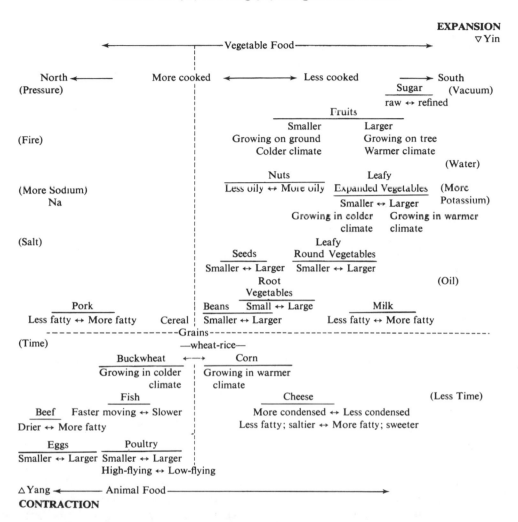

The above chart gives the general classification of food groups from yang to yin. However, more precise classification should be made upon examination of environmental conditions, nature and structure, chemical compounds, and effect upon our physical and mental conditions. Also, cooking can greatly change food qualities from yin to yang and yang to yin.

as the seasons change. Cooler, or more yin weather produces more contracting energy; warmer, or more yang weather produces more expansive energy. This same cycle can be applied to the part of the world in which a food originates. Foods that find their origin in hot tropical climates where the vegetation is lush and abundant are more expanded, while foods originating in northern or colder climates are more contracted.

We can also generally classify plants according to color, although there are often exceptions, from the more yin colors—violet, indigo, green, and white—through the more yang colors—yellow, brown, and red. And, as mentioned above, we should also consider the ratio of chemical components such as sodium, which is contractive, to potassium, which is expansive, in determining the quality of a particular food.

So far we have been discussing the different qualities of plant foods. Now let us consider the differences between plants and animals. For the most part, animal foods are classified as having more contracting energy. Why are plants more yin than animals? Well, for one, vegetables are generally immobile while animals move around actively. Plants also have a more expanded structure; their major portion branches upward and differentiates above the ground, while animals are more compact units with less external differentiation. Further, animals often have high body temperatures, while plants are cool. Plants are also represented by the color green, chlorophyll, while animals are manifested in the color red, hemoglobin. Plant foods have a more cooling and relaxing effect on the body, while animal foods have a more warming or constricting effect.

In the chart presented above, foods are arranged according to yin and yang. The foods at the lower left generally have a greater degree of contracting force. Those appearing closer to the center of the chart (represented by two intersecting lines of balance) have a more even balance of both forces, and those toward the upper right, a predominance of more expanding energy.

There is a tremendous range of variation within each category of food. Animal foods are generally more condensed than grains or vegetables, but among the many varieties of animal food, some are more contracting and others less so. Eggs, meat, and poultry, for example, have more extreme contracting energy than fish and other types of seafood. Among fish, those with red meat and blue skin are more extreme than white-meat varieties. Although dairy products come from an animal source, certain varieties—such as hard, salty cheeses—are more contracting, while others —such as yogurt, butter, ice cream, and cottage cheese—have a more expansive quality.

The quality of energy in cereal grains is generally more centrally balanced, and this is reflected nutritionally in the average proportion of minerals to protein to carbohydrate they contain. However, a wide range of energies can be found among grains, so that varieties such as buckwheat, millet, and winter wheat have a more contracting effect, while summer wheat, barley, and corn are more expansive. Brown rice is generally in-between, but again, this depends on the variety being considered. Short-grain rice, which is the most suitable variety for temperate climates, is generally the most balanced, followed by meduim- and long-grain varieties that are used more frequently in warmer areas.

Beans are generally more expanded than grains, but as with other categories of food, a wide range of variation exists among them. For example, certain varieties —including *azuki* beans, chick-peas, and lentils—are smaller and lower in fat. They have more balanced energy than beans which are relatively larger or higher in fat—such as pinto, kidney, and lima beans.

Azuki beans provide a good example of the way in which climate and environment influence the quality of a food. Some azuki beans have a shiny surface and a deep maroon color. They are grown in mineral-rich volcanic soil in the northern

Japanese island of Hokkaido, where the climate is similar to that of Maine. Other varieties have a somewhat faded color and a dull surface. They are grown in southern China, in a warmer climate. Either variety is fine for regular use, but for the recovery of health, the mineral-rich Hokkaido beans, which have stronger energy, are preferred.

Soybeans have strong expanding energy, and this is reflected in their high fat and protein content. If their expanding qualities are not rebalanced through cooking or natural processing, the beans can be difficult to digest. One way to rebalance the energy in soybeans is to mix them with grains such as rice or barley, and age them with sea salt and enzymes to produce a product such as miso. When used properly, miso strengthens digestion, while making balanced proteins and beneficial enzymes available to the body. Among fermented soybean products, those such as miso and tamari soy sauce are aged for a longer period and have more concentrated energy, while those such as tofu and soy milk, which are quickly processed from the more expanded liquid portion of the bean, have more expanding energy.

Sea vegetables generally have more concentrated energy than most land varieties, and this is reflected in their high mineral content. Those that grow closer to the shore or in warmer water are lighter and more expansive; those that grow in deeper, colder waters are more concentrated, as are those with a higher amount of minerals.

Vegetables generally have more expanding energy than grains or beans. As we saw in our comparison of foods, leafy green vegetables have more upward or rising energy; round-shaped vegetables—such as cabbage, onion, and squash—are more evenly balanced; and root vegetables are more contracted. However, aside from shape, size, and direction of growth, where a vegetable originates is a key factor in creating its energy quality. Vegetables such as tomato, potato, yams, avocado, eggplant, and peppers originated in South America or other tropical areas before being imported into Europe and North America. Compared to temperate varieties, like cabbage or kale, they have more extreme expanding energy, and for this reason, it is better for people in temperate zones to avoid using them.

In general, fruits have stronger expanding energy than vegetables. They are softer, sweeter, juicier, and composed of more simple sugar. The place of origin also plays a decisive role in creating the quality of energy in each variety of fruit. Tropical or semi-tropical fruits—including pineapple, banana, kiwi, and citrus—have more extreme expanding energy than apples, pears, peaches, melons, and others that grow in the temperate zones. As with vegetables that originate in the tropics, these more extreme varieties of fruit are also best avoided by persons who live in temperate zones.

A variety of foods have even more extreme energy. Concentrated sweeteners such as honey, maple syrup, and molasses are all very expansive, as are refined sugar and artificial sweeteners. Simple sugars are more fragmented or expansive than complex carbohydrates such as those in whole grains, beans, and local vegetables. Other products that originate in the tropics—such as spices, coffee, and chocolate—are also included in the more extreme yin category, as is alcohol. But many medications, including aspirin and antibiotics, and drugs such as marijuana and cocaine, are even further out on the energy spectrum. These products all have extremely expansive effects. A table in which foods are classified into extreme yang, more centrally balanced, and extreme yin categories, is presented below.

General Yin (▽) and Yang (△) Classification of Food

Strong Yang Foods
Refined salt
Eggs
Meat
Hard cheese
Chicken and poultry
Lobster, crab, and other shellfish
Red meat and blue-skinned fish

More Balanced Foods
Unrefined white sea salt, miso, tamari soy sauce, and other naturally salty seasonings
Tekka, gomashio, umeboshi, and other naturally processed salty condiments
Low fat, white-meat fish
Sea vegetables
Whole cereal grains
Beans and bean products

Root, round, and leafy green vegetables (from temperate climates)
Seeds and nuts (from temperate climates)
Temperate-climate fruit
Nonaromatic, nonstimulant beverages
Spring or well water
Naturally processed vegetable oils
Brown rice syrup, barley malt, and other natural grain-based sweeteners (when used moderately)

Strong Yin Foods
White rice, white flour
Frozen and canned foods
Tropical fruits and vegetables (including those originating in the tropics such as tomato and potato)
Milk, cream, yogurt, and ice cream
Refined oils
Spices (pepper, curry, nutmeg, etc.)
Aromatic and stimulant beverages (coffee, black tea, mint tea, etc.)
Honey, sugar, and refined sweeteners
Alcohol
Foods containing chemicals, preservatives, dyes, and pesticides
Artificial sweeteners
Drugs (marijuana, cocaine, etc., with some exceptions)
Medications (tranquilizers, antibiotics, etc., with some exceptions)

The items in this chart are generally listed from most yang to most yin. The foods in the more balanced column are generally recommended for consumption in temperate climates, while those in the strong yang and strong yin columns are generally not recommended as a part of a preventive lifestyle. Certain items within the centrally balanced column, such as sea salt and other seasonings, condiments, white-meat fish, seasonal fruits, oils, and concentrated sweeteners are used in small amounts only or consumed occasionally.

A Balanced Diet ———————————————————

An optimum diet is one that is well-balanced in terms of yin and yang. Human tooth structure reveals a general pattern of nourishment that is ideally suited to our requirements. Of the thirty-two adult teeth, twenty are molars or premolars. These are ideal for crushing and grinding grains, beans, seeds, and other fibrous plant foods. We also have eight front incisors, and these are ideal for cutting vegetables. The remaining four canine teeth—which are not sharply pointed in everyone—can be used for tearing animal food. A diet that matches this structure would ideally be composed of about five parts grain and other fibrous plant foods, two parts vegetables, and depending on climate and personal need, one part animal food. The ratio of animal food, which is more contracting, to plant food, which is more expanding, would average out to about one to seven. As we can see, the primary foods in the human diet would be those with more centrally balanced energy.

Traditional diets around the world reflect this pattern. For thousands of years, whole cereal grains, beans, and fresh local vegetables were eaten as staples. It was not until the twentieth century that the large-scale shift away from these traditional staples began. During this time, the rates of so-called degenerative diseases—especially heart disease and cancer—increased dramatically.

Prior to the twentieth century, most people based their diets around the foods that were naturally available to them. They ate in harmony with their climate and with the changing seasons. Their ecologically balanced diet afforded them maximum adaptability to the immediate environment.

Today however, people in the temperate zones eat what may be described as a "polar-tropical" diet. They have replaced the whole grains, beans, fresh local vegetables, and other foods appropriate to their region with meat, eggs, cheese, poultry, and other foods more suited to cold, polar climates, and with sugar, chocolate, spices, coffee, tropical fruits and vegetables, and other items more suited to equatorial zones.

Eating this way causes us to lose touch with the environment and can affect the body in any number of ways. In the circulatory system, for example, the arteries and blood vessels—which are normally open and flexible—can easily become clogged with deposits of fat and cholesterol. As the blood vessels become narrow and constricted, blood no longer flows smoothly through them. In some cases, the flow of blood to an organ or other part of the body can be cut off. When this happens in the blood vessels that supply the heart, the result is a heart attack. When it occurs in the blood vessels that supply the brain, the result is a stroke. Both conditions are common today because people eat a large volume of fatty animal food. As we can see, the overintake of extremes creates imbalance in the body.

The digestive organs are also affected by the overintake of extreme foods. The human digestive system—especially the large intestine—is much longer than that of carnivorous animals. It is ideally suited to the digestion of plant fibers. Animal foods decay more quickly than plant foods, and when they decay, they produce toxic compounds and bacteria. In carnivorous animals, waste products transit through the intestines quickly, and there is less time for toxins to build up. But the length of the human digestive tract allows ample time for toxic build-up to occur. Moreover, the hard fats contained in animal foods can also accumulate in the inner lining of the intestine, interfering with the smooth absorption and elimination of food. This often creates chronic constipation and the further build-up of toxic matter in a continual cycle.

In severe cases, this condition can produce cell changes that lead to cancer. Colon cancer, which is very common today, is frequently associated with diet; for example, people in countries with high intakes of animal fat and a low intake of fiber tend to have much higher rates of colon cancer than people in countries where the opposite dietary pattern prevails.

Yin and yang attract one another just as man and woman or the opposite poles of a magnet do. As consumption of foods with strong contracting energy increases, so does the desire for foods with strong expanding energy. Today people consume a large volume of sugar, tropical fruits, soft drinks, ice cream, chocolate, and other extremely yin foods in order to balance a high intake of animal products. The craving for sugar, chocolate, and other concentrated sweeteners, which many people now experience, is fueled by the overintake of foods with extremely contracting energy. These cravings are simply the result of opposites attracting.

Diabetes is an example of what can happen when the overintake of foods with strong expanding energy becomes excessive. The cells that produce insulin are located in the pancreas. Overconsumption of simple sugars, oils, fats, and other extremely expansive foods can cause these cells to become overexpanded and weak. In some cases, they lose the ability to secrete insulin, or if they are able to secrete this hormone, its quality may be too weak to effectively lower the level of sugar in the blood.

These are only several out of many examples of the way that overconsumption of extremes can lead to illness. The relationship between an extreme diet and degenerative sickness is now being recognized by public health agencies around the world. The high consumption of meat, eggs, cheese, poultry, sugar, chocolate, soft drinks, and refined and processed foods has been linked to cancer, high blood pressure, diabetes, various forms of heart disease, and even mental and psychological disorders. At the same time, the value of basing the diet around more centrally balanced complex carbohydrates—whole grains, beans, fresh vegetables, and local fruits—is also being increasingly recognized. The preventive dietary guidelines of the American Cancer Society, the American Heart Association, the National Academy of Sciences, and other leading public health organizations all point to these more centrally balanced foods as being essential in avoiding cancer, heart disease, and other degenerative sicknesses.

In this chapter, we have introduced the understanding of food in terms of energy quality, based on the view that everything in nature is a manifestation of universal energy. These dietary principles are centuries old, and are being increasingly supported by modern scientific and nutritional research. In the chapters that follow, we present guidelines for selecting the most balanced foods, and discuss the role of salad in a naturally balanced diet.

Chapter 2

Macrobiotic Eating

Unlike the modern diet, which is based on extremes, macrobiotic eating emphasizes foods and beverages that are more centrally balanced. In a temperate, or four-season climate, a macrobiotically balanced diet would emphasize the following:

1) More complex carbohydrates (centrally balanced) and fewer simple sugars (more extremely expansive);

2) More vegetable-quality protein (centrally balanced) and less protein from animal sources (more extremely contractive);

3) Less overall consumption of fat—more unsaturated fat (contained in centrally balanced whole grains, beans, and other vegetable foods) and less saturated fat (contained in more extreme animal foods);

4) Adequate consideration of the ideal balance between vitamins, minerals, and other nutritional factors (reflecting the overall balance between expanding and contracting energies required for human needs, while allowing for individual and climatic differences);

5) Use of more organically grown, natural-quality food and fewer chemically sprayed or fertilized items (chemical fertilizers and sprays are more extremely expansive—they diminish the energy of the foods they are used on);

6) Use of more traditionally processed foods and fewer artificially and chemically processed foods (artificial colorings, flavorings, and other additives are for the most part extremely expansive);

7) A larger intake of foods in their whole form and less intake of refined and partial foods (as we saw in the example of carrots and carrot greens, whole foods contain a more natural balance of expanding and contracting energies);

8) More consumption of foods rich in natural fiber rather than foods that have been devitalized (again, the energy in whole foods is more integrated and natural than that in refined or artificially processed foods).

These basic guidelines have been practiced daily for more than a quarter of a century by hundreds of thousands of people throughout the world, including many families. Moreover, similar dietary practices have been observed traditionally by many cultures for thousands of years.

The guidelines for food selection presented in this chapter are for people living in temperate climates. Modifications are required if you live in a tropical or subtropical climate, or a polar or semi-polar region. If we move north, for example, we need to increase the consumption of foods with stronger contracting energy, while de-emphasizing foods with stronger expanding energy. People who inhabit far-northern regions, such as the Eskimo, traditionally based their diets around animal food. Their way of eating was macrobiotic in the sense of being in harmony with the extreme climate in which they lived, since plant foods were largely unavailable to them.

We also need to adjust our diet when we travel or move to another climate. If we move to a warmer climate, we need to increase the intake of foods with more expanding energies, while decreasing those with more contracting energies. We also need to adjust our diet to accommodate the change in seasonal energy. This aspect will be discussed in the next chapter, including the importance of modifying our cooking technique to suit changes in temperature and weather. It is important to flexibly adapt these guidelines to suit everyone's individual needs and condition. No two people should, or can, eat the same diet. For this reason, it is a good idea to meet with a qualified macrobiotic teacher or to participate in educational programs such as the Macrobiotic Way of Life Seminar and the Macrobiotic Residential Seminar presented by the Kushi Foundation, in order to receive individual guidance as well as hands-on training in the basics of macrobiotic practice. (A schedule of these ongoing programs is available from the Kushi Foundation in Boston or Becket.)

Standard Macrobiotic Diet

The standard macrobiotic way of eating offers an incredible variety of foods and cooking methods to choose from. Its guidelines are broad and flexible. You can apply them when selecting the highest quality natural foods throughout the year.

Whole Cereal Grains

Whole cereal grains are the most centrally balanced foods in terms of expanding and contracting energies. This is why they have been traditionally thought of as the staff of life and why they are an essential part of a healthful way of eating today. It is much easier to balance the overall energy in your diet if your primary foods are centrally balanced. If you live in a temperate climate, whole grains may comprise up to 50 to 60 percent of daily intake. Below is a list of the whole grains and grain products that may be included:

Brown Rice
Brown rice—short, medium, and
   long grain
Genuine brown rice cream
Puffed brown rice
Brown rice flakes

Sweet Brown Rice
Sweet brown rice grain

Mochi (pounded sweet rice)
Sweet brown rice flour products

Barley
Barley grain
Pearl barley
Pearled barley
Puffed barley
Barley flour products

The Standard Macrobiotic Diet*

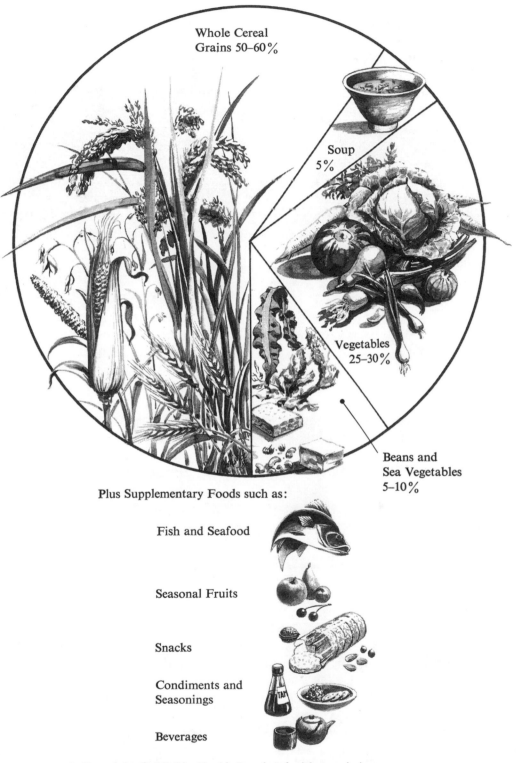

Whole Cereal
Grains 50–60%

Soup
5%

Vegetables
25–30%

Beans and
Sea Vegetables
5–10%

Plus Supplementary Foods such as:

Fish and Seafood

Seasonal Fruits

Snacks

Condiments and
Seasonings

Beverages

* Copyright © Michio Kushi. Reprinted with permission.

Whole Wheat
Whole wheat berries
Whole wheat bread
Whole wheat chapatis
Whole wheat noodles and pastas
Whole wheat flakes
Whole wheat flour
Whole wheat flour products such
  as crackers, matzos, muffins, etc.
Couscous
Bulgur
Fu (baked puffed wheat gluten)
Seitan (wheat gluten)

Millet
Millet grain
Millet flour products
Puffed millet

Oats
Whole oats
Steel-cut oats
Rolled oats
Oatmeal
Oat flakes

Oat flour products

Corn
Corn on the cob
Corn grits
Cornmeal
Arepas
Corn flour products such as bread,
  muffins, etc.
Puffed corn
Popped corn

Rye
Rye grain
Rye bread
Rye flakes
Rye flour products

Buckwheat
Buckwheat groats (kasha)
Buckwheat noodles (*soba*) and
  pastas
Buckwheat flour products such as
  pancakes, etc.

Cooked whole grains are preferable to flour products or to cracked or rolled grains because of easier digestibility. In general, it is better to keep intake of flour products—or cracked or rolled grains—to less than 15 to 20 percent of your daily whole-grain intake.

Soups

Soups may comprise about 5 percent of each person's daily intake. For most people, that averages out to about one or two cups or small bowls of soup per day, depending on individual desire and preference. Soups can include more centrally balanced vegetables, grains, beans, sea vegetables, noodles or other grain products, bean products like tofu, *tempeh*, and others, or occasionally, fish or seafood. Soups can be moderately seasoned with either miso, tamari soy sauce, sea salt, *umeboshi* plum or paste, or occasionally, ginger. Strongly expansive seasonings such as spices are best avoided in temperate climates.

Soups can be made thick and rich, or as simple clear broths. The texture of soups can vary with seasonal change and personal desire. Vegetable, grain, or bean stews can also be enjoyed, while a variety of garnishes, such as scallions, parsley, *nori* sea vegetable, and croutons may be used to enhance the appearance and flavor of soups.

Vegetables

Roughly one-quarter to one-third (25 to 30 percent) of each person's daily intake can include vegetables. Nature provides an incredible variety of local vegetables to choose from. For persons in temperate climates, the more centrally balanced vegetables that originate in the same climate are recommended. Vegetables that originate in the tropics have more extreme expansive energy and are best avoided. Some of those recommended for regular use include:

Acorn squash	Iceberg lettuce
Bok choy	*Jinenjo* (Japanese mountain potato)
Broccoli	Jerusalem artichoke
Burdock root	Kale
Buttercup squash	Kohlrabi
Butternut squash	Leeks
Cabbage	Lotus root
Celery	Mushrooms
Celery root	Mustard greens
Carrots	Onion
Carrot tops	Parsley
Cauliflower	Parsnips
Chinese cabbage	Pumpkin
Chives	Patty pan squash
Collard greens	Radish
Cucumber	Red cabbage
Daikon radish	Romaine lettuce
Daikon greens	Scallions
Dandelion greens	*Shiitake* mushrooms
Dandelion root	Snap beans
Endive	Summer squash
Escarole	Turnip
Green beans	Turnip greens
Green peas	Watercress
Hubbard squash	Wax beans
Hokkaido pumpkin	

Vegetables can be served in soups, or with grains, beans or sea vegetables. They can also be used in making rice rolls (macrobiotic *sushi*), served with noodles or pasta, cooked with fish, or served alone. The methods for cooking vegetables that are introduced in this book include boiling, steaming, pressing, sautéing (both waterless and with oil), and pickling. A variety of natural seasonings, including miso, tamari soy sauce, sea salt, and brown rice or umeboshi vinegar are recommended in vegetable cookery.

Beans

About 5 to 10 percent of daily meals may include beans or bean products. Beans that are smaller in size (such as azuki, chick-pea, and lentils) and contain less fat are more centrally balanced and are preferred for regular use. Persons in good overall health may select from any of the following:

Beans
Azuki beans
Black-eyed peas
Black turtle beans
Black soybeans
Chick-peas (garbanzo beans)
Great northern beans
Kidney beans
Lentils (green and red)
Lima beans
Mung beans
Navy beans
Pinto beans
Soybeans
Split peas

Whole dried peas
Bean sprouts

Bean Products
Dried tofu (soybean curd that has been naturally dried)
Fresh tofu
Okara (pulp or residue left from making tofu)
Natto (fermented soybeans)
Yuba (dried soy milk)
Tempeh (fermented soybeans or combination of soybeans and grains)

Beans and bean products are more easily digested when cooked with a small volume of seasonings such as sea salt, miso, or *kombu* sea vegetable. They may also be prepared with vegetables, chestnuts, dried apples, or raisins, or occasionally sweetened with grain sweeteners like barley malt and rice honey. Beans and bean products may be served in soups and side dishes, or cooked with grains or sea vegetables.

Sea Vegetables

Sea vegetables may be used daily in cooking. Side dishes can be made with *arame* or *hijiki* and included several times per week. *Wakame* and kombu can be used daily in miso and other soups, in vegetable and bean dishes, or as condiments. Toasted nori is also recommended for daily or regular use, while agar-agar can be used from time to time in making a natural jelled dessert known as *kanten* (agar-agar also has natural laxative properties). Below is a list of the sea vegetables for use in macrobiotic cooking:

Arame
Agar-agar
Dulse
Hijiki

Irish moss
Kombu
Nori
Wakame

Fish and Seafood

Fish and seafood have more contracting energy than most vegetable foods. They can be eaten on occasion to supplement the foods listed above. Amounts eaten can vary, depending upon each person's needs and desires, but generally, fish can be eaten several times per week as a part of a balanced meal. White-meat varieties that are lowest in saturated fat and most easily digested are recommended for regular use.

Regular Use	*Occasional Use*
Carp	Cherrystone clams
Cod	Littleneck clams
Small dried fish (*iriko*)	Crab
Flounder	Oyster
Haddock	Lobster
Halibut	Shrimp
Herring	
Scrod	*Infrequent Use*
Dried fish	Bluefish
Smelt	Salmon
Snapper	Sardines
Sole	Swordfish
Trout	Tuna
Other white-meat fish	Other blue-skinned and red-meat fish

Garnishes are especially important in balancing fish and seafood. Recommended garnishes include: chopped scallions or parsley, grated raw daikon, ginger, radish, or horseradish, grated green Japanese horseradish, called *wasabi*, raw salad, and shredded daikon.

Fruit

Fruits have more expanding energy than most grains, beans, and temperate vegetables. In most cases, fruit can be enjoyed three or four times per week. Locally grown or temperate-climate fruits are preferable, while tropical fruits—which are extremely expansive—are not recommended for regular use for people in temperate regions. Below are some of the varieties of fruit for consumption in temperate climates:

Apples	Lemons
Apricots	Mulberries
Blackberries	Persimmon
Cantaloupe	Peaches
Grapes	Plums
Honeydew melon	Raisins

Raspberries	Watermelon
Strawberries	Wild berries
Tangerines	

Pickles

Pickles can be eaten frequently as a supplement to main dishes. They stimulate appetite and help digestion. Some varieties—such as pickled daikon, or *takuan*—can be bought prepackaged in natural food stores. Others—such as quick pickles—can be prepared at home. Certain varieties take just a few hours to prepare, while others require more time.

A wide variety of pickles are fine for regular use, including salt, salt brine, bran, miso, tamari soy sauce, umeboshi vinegar, and others. Sauerkraut may also be used in small volume on a regular basis.

Seeds and Nuts

Seeds and nuts can be eaten from time to time as snacks and garnishes. They can be roasted with or without sea salt, sweetened with barley or rice malt, or seasoned with tamari soy sauce. Seeds and nuts can be ground into butter, shaved and served as a topping, garnish, or ingredient in various dishes, including dessert. Below are varieties that can be used:

Nuts (More Regular Use)	Macadamia nuts
Almonds	Others
Chestnuts	
Filberts	*Seeds*
Peanuts	Black and white sesame seeds
Pecans	Pumpkin seeds
Pine nuts	Squash seeds
Small Spanish nuts	Sunflower seeds
Walnuts	Poppy seeds
	Umeboshi plum seeds
Nuts (Infrequent Use)	Alfalfa seeds
Brazil nuts	Others
Cashews	

Snacks

A variety of natural snacks may be enjoyed from time to time, including those made from whole grains, like cookies, bread, puffed cereals, mochi, rice cakes, rice balls, and macrobiotic sushi. Nuts and seeds may also be used as snacks, for example by roasting them with sea salt, tamari soy sauce, or sweetening them with grain-based sweeteners.

Condiments

A variety of condiments may be used, some daily and others occasionally. Small amounts can be sprinkled on foods to adjust taste and nutritional value, and to stimulate appetite. They can be used on grains, soups, vegetables, beans, and sometimes desserts. The most frequently used varieties include:

Gomashio (roasted sesame seeds and sea salt)
Sea vegetable powders (with or without roasted sesame seeds)
Tekka (a special condiment made with soybean miso, sesame oil, burdock, lotus root, carrots, and ginger)
Umeboshi (pickled salt) plums

Condiments That Can Be Used Occasionally:
Roasted sesame seeds
Roasted and chopped *shiso* (pickled beefsteak plant) leaves
Shio kombu (kombu cooked with tamari soy sauce and water)
Green nori flakes
Cooked nori condiment
Cooked miso with scallions or onions
Umeboshi or brown rice vinegar

Seasonings

A variety of seasonings can be used when cooking macrobiotically. It is better to avoid strong expansive seasonings such as curry, hot pepper, and other spices, and to use those which are naturally processed from vegetable products or natural sea salt, and which have been in use as a part of traditional diets. These traditional seasonings have more centrally balanced energy when used in small amounts. A list of seasonings is presented below:

Unrefined sea salt
Soy sauce
Tamari soy sauce (fermented soybean and grain sauce)
Miso (fermented soybean and grain paste, e.g., rice, barley, soybean, sesame, and other misos)
Brown rice and umeboshi vinegar
Barley malt and rice syrup
Grated daikon, radish, and ginger
Umeboshi plum and paste
Lemon, tangerine, and orange juice
Green and yellow mustard paste
Sesame, corn, safflower, mustard seed, and olive oil
Mirin (fermented sweet brown rice sweetener)
Amazaké (fermented sweet brown rice beverage)
Other traditional natural seasonings

Garnishes

A variety of garnishes can be used to create balance among dishes and facilitate digestion. The use of garnishes depends upon the needs and desires of each person. The following garnishes can be used:

> Grated daikon (for fish, mochi, noodles, and other dishes)
> Grated radish (used like grated daikon)
> Grated horseradish (used mostly for fish and seafood)
> Chopped scallions (for noodles, fish, and seafood, etc.)
> Parsley
> Lemon, tangerine, and orange slices (mainly for fish and seafood)
> Others

Desserts

A variety of natural desserts may be eaten from time to time, usually at the end of the main meal. Desserts can be made from azuki beans (sweetened with grain syrup, chestnuts, squash, or raisins); cooked or dried fruit; agar-agar (natural sea-vegetable gelatin); grains (e.g., rice pudding, couscous cake, Indian pudding, etc.); and flour products (e.g., cookies, cakes, pies, muffins, etc., prepared with fruit or grain sweeteners).

Beverages

A variety of beverages may be consumed daily or occasionally. Amounts can vary according to each person's needs and weather conditions. Soft drinks, frozen orange juice, coffee, commercial tea, and other drinks with more extreme expanding energy are best avoided. The beverages listed below can be used to comfortably satisfy the desire for liquid.

> *Bancha* twig and stem tea
> Roasted brown rice or barley tea
> Cereal-grain coffee
> Spring or well water
> Amazaké
> Dandelion tea
> Soybean milk (prepared with kombu)
> Kombu tea
> Lotus root tea
> *Mu* tea
> Other traditional nonstimulant and nonaromatic natural herbal beverages
> *Saké* (fermented rice wine, without chemicals or sugar)
> Beer (more natural quality)
> Apple, grape, and apricot juice

Apple cider
Carrot, celery, and other vegetable juices

Additional Foods

In some cases, the standard macrobiotic diet can be temporarily modified to include other foods. These modifications can be made according to individual requirements and necessity; though within usual practice, additional foods are usually not necessary for the maintenance of health and well-being.

Suggestions for Healthy Living

Together with eating well, there are a number of practices that we recommend for a healthier and more natural life. Practices such as keeping physically active and using natural cooking utensils, fabrics, and materials in the home are especially recommended. These practices help us maintain harmony with the environment. In the past, people lived more closely with nature and ate a more balanced, natural diet. With each generation, we have gotten further and further from our roots in nature, and have experienced a corresponding increase in cancer and other chronic illnesses. The suggestions presented below complement a balanced natural diet and can help everyone enjoy more satisfying and harmonious living.

- Live each day happily without being worried about your health. Keep active mentally and physically. Sing every day and encourage others to join with you.
- Greet everyone and everything with gratitude, particularly offering thanks before and after each meal. Encourage others to give thanks for their food and their natural environment.
- Try to get to bed before midnight and get up early in the morning.
- Try not to wear synthetic clothing or woolen articles directly against your skin. Wear cotton instead. Keep jewelry and accessories simple, natural, and graceful.
- If you are able, go outdoors in simple clothing every day. When the weather permits, walk barefoot on grass, soil, or beach. Go on regular outings, especially to beautiful natural areas.
- Keep your home clean and orderly. Make your kitchen, bathroom, bedrooms, and living rooms shiny clean. Keep the atmosphere of your home bright and cheerful.
- Maintain an active correspondence. Express love and appreciation to your parents, husband or wife, children, brothers, sisters, relatives, friends, and associates.
- Try not to take long hot baths or showers unless you have been consuming too much salt or animal food.
- Every morning or every night, scrub your whole body with a hot, moist towel

until your circulation becomes active. When a complete body-scrub is not convenient, at least do your hands, feet, fingers, and toes.

- Use natural cosmetics, soaps, shampoos, and body care products. Brush your teeth with natural preparations or sea salt.
- Keep as active as you can. Daily activities such as cooking, scrubbing floors, cleaning windows, washing clothes, and others are excellent forms of exercise. You may also try systematic exercises such as yoga, martial arts, aerobics, and sports.
- Try to minimize time spent in front of the television. Color television especially emits unnatural radiation that can be physically draining. Turn the television off during mealtimes. Balance television with more productive activities.
- Switch from electric to gas cooking at the earliest convenience. Microwave cooking is best avoided.
- Heating pads, electric blankets, portable radios with earphones, and other electric devices can disrupt the body's natural flow of energy. They are not recommended for regular use.
- Put many green plants in your living room, bedroom, and throughout the house to freshen and enrich the air.

The way in which we eat can be just as important as the choice of foods. Regular meals are better, and be sure to include a whole-grain dish at each meal (the word "meal" actually means "crushed whole grain"). The amount of food eaten depends on each person's needs. Snacking is best kept moderate, so that it does not replace meals, while tea and other beverages can be enjoyed throughout the day as desired.

Chewing is also very important; try to chew each mouthful of food until it becomes liquid. Thorough chewing allows for the efficient digestion and absorption of foods. Moreover, chewing mixes food with saliva, a natural substance that helps protect the body from infection. In fact, in a study published in the May, 1988 issue of the *Journal of the American Dental Association*, researchers found that saliva can prevent the AIDS virus from infecting white blood cells.

You can eat whenever you feel hungry, but try to avoid eating before bedtime, preferably for three hours, except in unusual circumstances. Finally, learn to appreciate your foods and the health-giving properties they contain. Let your gratitude overflow to include nature, the universe, and all of the people who live on this wonderful planet.

Chapter 3

The Yin and Yang of Salad

Every plant should bear its part without being overpower'd by some Herb of stronger taste, so as to endanger the native Savor and Vertue of the rest; but fall into their places like Notes in Music, in which should be nothing harsh or grating and tho admitting some discords (to distinguish and illustrate the next) striking in the more sprightly and sometimes gentler notes reconcile all dissonances and melt them into an agreeable composition.

John Evelyn
Acteria, *A Discourse of Sallets*, 1699

As the seventeenth century English diarist and horticulturist noted above, successful salad making depends on the proper balance of ingredients. The same principle applies to cooking in general: successful cooking depends on how well we harmonize the ingredients in each dish and the various dishes in a meal.

A similar concept exists in the Far East. The Japanese dishes *sunomono* and *aemono* are traditional equivalents of salads. Their names mean "vinegared" and "dressed" things. Aemono also refers to foods that have been "combined," "composed," or "harmonized," reflecting the ideal of achieving harmony and balance in each dish.

Practically all of the balanced natural foods listed in the previous chapter can be harmoniously blended into colorful and delicious salads. Salads can be used to supplement regular cooked dishes and can include whole grains, beans and bean products, sea and land vegetables, fish and seafood, seasonal fruits, and nuts and seeds. Macrobiotic condiments and seasonings can also be used in preparing dressings. With such a wide range of healthfully balanced foods and seasonings to choose from, your salads can be endlessly varied and interesting.

Before we discuss the role of salad in a naturally balanced diet, let us look a little more closely at the difference between cooked and uncooked foods, and see how cooking changes the energy in food.

Rebalancing Food Energy

When we cook or process food in some way, we change the quality of its energy. How the food is cooked determines the way in which its energy changes.

Fire and water are the primary influences used in cooking. Each of these factors changes food in a way that is opposite to the other. Fire has a more contracting effect. If we place a food over an open flame, it becomes drier and more contracted, and eventually turns into ashes. Water has the opposite effect. It draws the minerals out of foods, causing them to become softer and more expanded.

If we roast grains, beans, or seeds in a dry skillet, they become harder, drier, and darker in color. When fire is the only factor used—as it is in dry-roasting—the food becomes more contracted. On the other hand, soaking a food in water will change it in the opposite way. It will expand and eventually decompose.

In cooking, we balance these opposite energies. Cooking can be thought of as a form of predigestion in which food is energized and partially broken down, so that we are better able to extract energy and nutrients from it.

Methods such as boiling, steaming, and pressure-cooking combine these opposite energies to varying degrees: the drying and contracting effects of fire are somewhat counterbalanced by the expanding effects of water or steam. Fire energizes food by accelerating the movement of atoms and molecules, so that cells break down and recombine in more concentrated form.

The crispness or hardness of raw plant foods is caused by water pressure inside the cells. This pressure causes the cellulose that makes up the outer cell wall to assume a more rigid structure. Heat causes these water molecules to expand and rupture the outer cell wall and coagulates the protein molecules in the cells. The cells become softer and more contracted, like a balloon does when the air is let out of it. Meanwhile, water offsets these contracting effects by keeping the food moist. It prevents food from becoming dried out or burnt.

The skillful cook stops the cooking process at just the right time, before the water evaporates and food becomes burnt and contracted, but not before it is adequately softened, broken down, and condensed. Here we can see that the amount of time that something is cooked influences its quality. The longer we cook it, the more concentrated it becomes. So, quickly boiled or steamed greens still retain freshness and crispness, while those that are cooked for a longer time become softer and less crispy.

Pressure-cooking, which is the most common method of cooking brown rice in most macrobiotic households, is a more concentrated form of boiling. It reduces the loss of minerals and other nutrients that would escape in steam during the boiling process. Pressure is a more contracting factor, squeezing moisture from foods and making them more concentrated.

A pinch of sea salt, or a small amount of miso, tamari soy sauce, umeboshi plum, or other natural seasoning is usually added during cooking. The minerals in sea salt cause foods to contract, somewhat counterbalancing the expanding effects of water or steam. Methods of cooking that combine the contracting effects of fire, salt, pressure, and time with the expanding effects of water are generally more balanced than methods like dry-roasting or grilling. Vegetable foods become sweeter, softer, and more energized when cooked in a more balanced manner.

Baking is also a more contracting method of cooking. When grains are baked, they are first crushed into flour. This fragments and disperses their energy. Then, water is added to make dough, further adding to the expansive quality of the flour. However, the dough is then placed in an enclosed oven and baked until it hardens. Baking causes the flour to become harder and drier, and accelerates its contracting energy. That is why overintake of baked flour products can make someone become drier, tighter, and crave liquids.

Drying or pickling foods also accelerates their contracting energy. If we compare fresh and dried apples, we see that the dried apples have lost much of their moisture and their sweetness has become more concentrated. If we compare fresh daikon with daikon that has been combined with rice bran and sea salt and aged for several years, as it is in takuan pickles, we see that pickling makes the daikon become harder, drier, saltier, and more contracted. On the other hand, oil creates expansive and upward energy. Only a small amount is needed from time to time to conduct heat and release the energy in food. On average, high-quality sesame oil is used in sautéing two to three times per week in most marcobiotic households.

Cooking and food processing allow us to rebalance the energy in food to suit our needs and desires. We can summarize the effects of the factors used in cooking and natural food processing as follows:

Yin Energy Is Accelerated by	*Yang Energy Is Accelerated by*
Lower temperatures (less fire)	Higher temperatures (more fire)
More water	Less water
Less salt	More salt
Less use of pressure	Greater use of pressure
Shorter cooking times	Longer cooking times
Freshness	Aging
More use of oil	Less or no use of oil
Soaking	Drying
Greater bacterial or yeast activity (i.e., fermentation)	Less bacterial or yeast activity

Variety, not only in the foods we cook, but in the methods we use to cook them, is an important element in a healthful way of eating. During the course of a day, we recommend that you use a variety of cooking methods. For example, you may wish to pressure-cook your main brown rice dish; use both quick and slow boiling for soups, beans, and vegetable dishes; blanch or steam your greens; and serve fermented pickles, pressed vegetables, or occasional raw salads. Moreover, condiments such as gomashio and sea-vegetable powders are prepared by roasting and crushing the ingredients. A wide range of cooking styles helps each person receive a well-balanced mix of food energies.

Changing with Climate and Season ——————

As the seasons change, so does the emphasis of our cooking. During the hot summer, we highlight factors that create more yin energy in our meals. For example, we may serve fresher, lighter dishes, including salads, and dishes that produce cooling effects, although iced foods and drinks are not recommended for health.

We may also pressure-cook less, and alternate this way of preparing brown rice with boiling. Modifications such as these are also appropriate in warm climates. For example, people who live in hot, dry places such as Arizona or Texas need not pressure-cook their rice throughout the year, and need not use short-grain brown rice as often as people who live in temperate climates. During the hot, dry season, they can boil (and pressure-cook occasionally), and can use medium- and long-grain rices. During the winter, or cooler season, pressure-cooked short-grain rice can be used more often, and these other rices and cooking methods can be used on occasion.

In colder or temperate climates, heartier, warming dishes are preferred during the winter. The factors that accelerate warming or contracting energy are appro-

Seasonal Modification Chart

These are general guidelines. Please adapt them flexibly to meet individual circumstances. Other foods and cooking methods not mentioned in the table can also be used. For the most part, seasonal modifications are subtle and gradual.

Season	Modifications
Spring	Lighter cooking methods; slightly less seasoning; slightly more fermented foods—tempeh, natto, amazaké, sauerkraut, light pickles, and pressed salads; slightly more sprouts and leafy greens; slightly more barley, wheat or wheat products; more boiling, steaming and quick sautéing
Summer	Simple cooking methods—boiling, steaming, quick sautéing; less cooking time; variety of fresh produce—leafy greens, corn on the cob, summer fruits; avoid cold or ice cold items; variety of noodle, grain, vegetable, bean and sea-vegetable salads; less oil; less seasoning
Autumn	Richer, well-cooked dishes; slightly longer cooking time; stews, soups; sautéing; sweet rice and mochi dishes; round sweet vegetables such as squash, pumpkin, turnips, onions, carrots, cabbage, etc.; slightly more oil; slightly more seasoning; rich, hearty flavors; variety of colors
Winter	Warm, stronger food; slightly more oil and seasoning; longer cooking methods—nishime, long sautéing, boiling, baking, etc.; fried noodle and grain dishes more often; more creamy, thick or rich soups and stews; warming desserts

From *Macrobiotic Family Favorites* by Aveline Kushi and Wendy Esko, Japan Publications, Inc., 1987.

priate under these circumstances. Spring and fall are seasons of transition, in which the emphasis in cooking needs to change to match the changing energy in the environment. In spring, energy is becoming lighter and more active as temperatures become warmer and the amount of sunlight increases. To balance these conditions, our cooking needs to change from an emphasis on the hearty, warming foods of winter to an emphasis on lighter, fresher dishes. At the opposite side of the cycle, in autumn, cooler temperatures create more condensed atmospheric energy. At this time of year, we can begin to emphasize the factors that help the body generate and store heat, in order to balance the environment and prepare for the coming winter.

In the above chart, general guidelines are presented for cooking with the changing seasons. Keep in mind that the overall balance between expanding and contracting energies in our cooking and choice of foods is generally the same throughout the year, and that seasonal variations are subtle. For example, so as to avoid one-sided cooking, we may still serve lightly steamed greens and blanched vegetables in winter, and well-cooked grain, bean, or vegetable dishes in summer. Although each season requires a slightly different emphasis, winter cooking should not be completely different than summer cooking, and vice versa. Learning to make the appropriate seasonal changes in your cooking requires sensitivity to personal needs and environmental conditions. Guidelines such as those presented above are flexible and dynamic, and their adaptation depends upon each circumstance. (Readers who would like further information about seasonal cooking may consult *Aveline Kushi's Introducing Macrobiotic Cooking*, Japan Publications, Inc., 1987, and the *Changing Seasons Macrobiotic Cookbook*, Avery Publishing Group, 1985, by the authors.)

Salad as a Balancing Factor

Actually, salads are not limited to servings of raw vegetables, although in modern times, that is what they often contain. The word "salad" comes from the Latin *herba salata*, or "salted greens," signifying that originally, vegetables were salted before being eaten as salad.

Writing in the American classic, *The Joy of Cooking*, authors Irma S. Rombauer and Marion Rombauer Becker state that salads were "originally . . . the edible parts of various herbs or plants dressed only with salt—from which the word salad comes." These original salads were more like the "pressed salads" used today in macrobiotic cooking. They were also similar to the Japanese sunomono, or "vinegared things." Processing raw vegetables in salt or traditional salty vinegar is an intuitive way of making balance: the contracting energy of salt balances the expanding energy of raw vegetables; it draws water from the vegetables and makes them softer and easier to digest.

In some cultures, especially those in warmer regions, salads were sometimes dressed with oil and vinegar in addition to salt. This practice goes back at least to

Greek times, when olive oil was used, and in most restaurants today, oil and vinegar are still served with salads. Oil and vinegar, which are yin, serve to balance the salt and lubricate the rough plant fibers, thus making them more palatable. These dressings cause osmotic pressure to build outside the cells, weakening their ability to hold water. The vegetables thus become softer and easier to digest. Traditionally processed vinegars, which are used in macrobiotic dressings and in "pressing" vegetables, also help facilitate digestion by initiating quick fermentation, which makes the vegetable fibers decompose slightly. However, in macrobiotic thinking, oil is too extreme to be eaten raw—except very occasionally by those in good health—and in the long term, can weaken our condition. Modern commercial vinegars are also more extreme, and are not recommended for regular use.

Actually, the human digestive system is not well-suited to digesting a large volume of raw plant foods, although some can be included from time to time if we are in good health. Cellulose, the tough fiber of plants, is not easily broken down in the human digestive tract. This contrasts with cows, deer, goats, buffalo, and other *ruminants*, who have an extensive fermentation system—the *rumen*—located at the beginning of their digestive tract. Here, bacteria break the tough plant fibers down into smaller molecules, so that nutrients can be efficiently absorbed. Human beings lack this digestive organ, and invented methods such as cooking, pickling, and fermentation to begin the breakdown of plant foods outside the body.

These natural methods of food processing are quite ancient. Cooking may have started as far back as a million years ago when our prehistoric ancestors sought to adapt to the increasing coldness brought on by the ice ages. Before that, early humanity may have subsisted largely on uncooked grains, vegetables, and other plant foods. Without fire, they had less adaptability to changes in the weather and climate. They may have lived only in the warmer zones of the earth, and migrated whenever their climate became colder. Fire gave humanity the potential to adapt to any climate on earth, and together with the discovery of salt, signaled the beginning of culture and civilization.

Why then, if cooked foods were the primary staples for so many thousands of years, are raw salads so popular today? The energy of raw vegetables is more expanded than that of cooked vegetables, and that is why salt was and still is used in processing them. Raw salads have an expanding and cooling effect on the body and help balance the contractive, heat-producing effects of meat, eggs, cheese, poultry, and other forms of animal food. The rise in popularity of raw salads (and of icy cold foods and drinks) is a result of the steady increase in the consumption of beef, chicken, cheese, and other animal foods that occurred in this century. It is logical therefore, that restaurants that specialize in grilled beef would start to offer raw salads. Yang attracts yin and yin attracts yang. The more we consume foods with strong contracting energy (yang), the more we seek those with strong expanding energy (yin) to make balance. This is the order of the universe.

This balancing principle also helps explain why tomatoes, green peppers, potatoes, various spicy herbs, and other foods from the tropics have become increasingly popular in modern cooking, and are often used in salads. These vegetables are far more expansive than those originating in temperate climates, and also help to neutralize the strong contractive energy in meat and other animal foods. However, an extreme balance between expanding and contracting energies in the diet often leads to imbalance in the body. So, for example, researchers have recently discovered that overconsumption of tomatoes, potatoes, and other vegetables in the *nightshade* family may contribute to demineralization of the bones and to arthritis.

In the modern diet, raw fruits and vegetables are often the closest thing to fresh or unprocessed foods that many people eat. As Margaret Visser states in *Much Depends on Dinner*, "Lettuce is often the only green vegetable on the menu, and for many people, it may be the only greenstuff commonly found in their diet." During the past sixty years, overall consumption of fresh vegetables and fruits —both commonplace in traditional diets—plummeted, while the intake of canned, frozen, and processed vegetables and fruits skyrocketed. As the modern diet became widespread, people came to rely less on fresh farm or backyard produce and more on factory produced foods. The desire for fresh salad is simply a way of making balance with a diet that is devoid of freshness and high in artifically processed foods. At the same time, the modern diet relies heavily on more intensive cooking methods that employ high heat, including grilling, charcoal broiling, and deep-frying. These energy-intensive methods also create the desire for fresh, cooling foods such as raw salads and fruits, including tropical varieties.

Fortunately, macrobiotics has revived the traditional reliance on fresh produce, and the use of more peaceful, natural cooking methods. With plenty of fresh, lightly cooked vegetables on hand, one becomes less attracted to raw foods. However, when the only vegetables we eat are those that come from a can or are thawed from a package, we naturally seek plenty of fresh raw salad or fruit.

During this century, the concept of salad underwent a complete turnaround. While traditional cooks made raw vegetables more yang through the use of salt, pressure, and other contracting factors (traditional people would also sprinkle a pinch of salt on watermelon or other fruit before eating it or soak apples, pears, and others in salt water), modern cooks began preparing sweetened salads. The invention of sugared, powdered gelatin in the 1890s accelerated this trend. Housewives soon began creating sugary gelatin salads that included items such as canned and fresh fruit, coconuts, whipped cream, and marshmallows. All of these ingredients are extremely yin, and these dishes are more like sugary desserts than salads. Like sugary desserts, these more extreme combinations can have detrimental effects on our health.

Salads in the Macrobiotic Diet ————————

Macrobiotic salads are more like the original *herba salata* than these modern concoctions are. Sugared gelatin, whipped cream, and tropical fruits are not used, nor are cheese, strong spices, potatoes, eggs, or tomatoes. A wide variety of cooked and uncooked ingredients can be included in macrobiotic salads, and they can be served as supplements to your regularly cooked dishes throughout the year.

In general, cooked salad dishes can be served more often than raw salads; the frequency depends upon the ingredients used and the season the dish is served in. General guidelines for including the varieties of salad introduced in this book as a part of the Standard Macrobiotic Diet are presented below:

1. **Whole-grain or whole-grain-pasta salads**—In warm or hot weather, these lightly cooked salad dishes can be served several times per week, along with other daily grain dishes. In winter or during cold weather, they can be included on occasion to add variety and lightness to meals.

2. **Vegetable salads and aspics**—Lightly blanched vegetables (known in macrobiotics as "boiled salads") can be served daily or often throughout the year, together with a wide variety of cooked-vegetable dishes. A small daily serving of vegetables that are pressed or pickled in sea salt or natural vinegar can also be included year round. Vegetable aspics, made with a natural, non-sugared sea vegetable gelatin known as agar-agar, can be served throughout the year; as often as several times per week during the warm weather.

   The upward energy (and cooling effect) of raw salad is most appropriate during the spring and summer. In the past, raw salads were often served as "spring tonics" to loosen stagnation caused by months of heavy winter cooking. The *Discourse of Sallets* mentions this seasonal aspect in a passage that describes how salads should change with the seasons: ". . . change your Standard; In Summer you ought to resemble a green tree; in Autumn a Castle carved out of Carrots and Turnips; in the Winter, a tree hanged with Snow."

   In general, raw salads can be eaten several times per week by persons in good health. This frequency can be increased somewhat during warm weather or if we live in a hot climate. However, persons with digestive or other health problems—especially those caused by overconsumption of more extreme yin foods and drinks—may need to temporarily limit or avoid the intake of raw salad (and other raw foods) until their condition improves. We recommend that persons with serious illness, including cancer, diabetes, immune deficiencies, and others, meet with a qualified macrobiotic teacher or attend an introductory program such as the Macrobiotic Way of Life Seminar presented in Boston for individual advice and guidance.

3. **Bean and tofu salads and aspics**—These cooked dishes can be included several times per week throughout the year. However, it is recommended that raw tofu salads be used only on occasion, and not by those with serious health problems, unless otherwise indicated. Bean sprouts are usually included in raw-vegetable salads, and can be served according to the recommendations presented above.

4. **Sea-vegetable salads and aspics**—These lightly cooked dishes can be included occasionally in cooler weather and up to several times per week in hot weather. They can be included as part of the regular consumption of sea vegetables.

5. **Fruit salad and kanten**—In general, a small volume of temperate-climate fruit can be consumed three to four times per week by persons in good

health. Tropical or semi-tropical fruits are not recommended for persons who live in temperate climates. Usually, fruits are cooked in dessert or eaten dried, with the consumption of raw fruit kept occasional. Fruit salads can be served once or twice a week during hot weather or in warm climates, while fruit kanten, a deliciously healthful alternative to sugared gelatin dessert, can be served several times per week during hot weather or in warm regions. Kanten is made with agar-agar, a natural sea vegetable gelatin, and can be served slightly chilled or at room temperature.

As with raw vegetables, the intake of raw fruit is a highly individual issue and depends upon the condition of each person's health. Those with serious illness are advised to contact a macrobiotic educational center for personal guidance and advice.

6. **Salad dressings**—Although macrobiotic salads can be eaten as is, dressings and condiments can be used on them from time to time. In general, macrobiotic condiments, such as umeboshi plum or paste, umeboshi or brown rice vinegar, toasted sesame seeds, and others can be used several times per week in preparing salad dressings, or in making pressed salads or pickles. Lightly toasted sunflower seeds can also be used as a garnish for salads, but because of their high oil content, are best used only occasionally. Croutons, made from whole grain breads, can also be used on occasion to garnish salads. As mentioned previously, plain, raw oil or commercial vinegar are generally not recommended for use on salads.

The salads, dressings, and other dishes presented in this book are made with natural ingredients. They add freshness and lightness to meals and can be included as a part of a balanced, healthful diet. Readers who would like more information on macrobiotic cooking and meal planning in general are invited to consult the cookbooks listed in the bibliography, or to attend macrobiotic cooking classes presented at educational centers throughout the United States and abroad.

We can also divide the types of salad (including kantens and aspics) into three categories:

1. **Simple salads, aspics, or kantens**—those which include from one to three ingredients.
2. **Mixed salads, aspics, or kantens**—those which are made with more than three ingredients.
3. **Crudités**—these are finger foods, usually vegetables, that are boiled, blanched, pickled, or eaten raw with a dip.

Simple salads, aspics, or kantens go well with more elaborate meals, while mixed salads are often best with simpler fare. Crudités are often served at parties, buffet, or special occasions, and are usually eaten as snacks before the main meal.

The preparation of macrobiotic salads, aspics, and kantens can involve a variety of cooking methods in addition to serving the ingredients raw. These include:

Boiling—This cooking method can be used for vegetable, bean and bean product, grain, sea vegetable, fruit, and fish or seafood salads.

Blanching—This method of very quick boiling is used primarily for vegetables and garnishes, including nuts.

Pressure-cooking—This method is used primarily for preparing brown rice and occasionally other grains used in salad. Beans can also be pressure-cooked on occasion.

Steaming—This method is used mainly for preparing vegetables.

Pressing and pickling—These methods are used primarily in preparing vegetables and occasionally fruits.

Deep-frying—This method is used mainly in the preparation of croutons which are added as garnish to salads.

Roasting—This method is used in preparing seed and nut garnishes, as well as in preparing dressings, croutons, and condiments.

Raw—Uncooked salads are usually simple, and include vegetables and fruits.

Before You Cook

Before you actually start cooking, a few suggestions on how to get your foods ready might be helpful. Let us first consider how to wash foods (a list of utensils is presented in the Glossary at the back of the book).

Washing grains, beans, and seeds—Before washing these foods, place a handful at a time on a plate and sort out any stones, clumps of soil, badly damaged beans, sticks or other debris. Then place grains, beans, or seeds in a bowl, covering them with cold water. Wash them quickly (this helps retain nutrients), using one hand to stir in one direction. Pour off the water and repeat once or twice more until the water is clean. Next, place the grain, beans, or seeds in a colander or wire-mesh strainer appropriate for their size, and quickly rinse thoroughly under cold water to remove any remaining dust. Allow to drain for a minute or so. The grains, beans, or seeds are now ready to use.

Washing sea vegetables—Most sea vegetables are washed in much the same manner as above, although there are exceptions. Kombu needs only to be lightly dusted off with a clean, damp sponge before soaking. Nori that is pressed into sheet form does not require washing; just simply toast and use. Regular dried nori that is not in sheet form must be washed.

Before washing, place the sea vegetable on a plate and sort out any hard clumps, stones, or shells, and discard them. Next, place the sea vegetable in a bowl and cover with cold water. Rinse quickly with one hand in one direction. Pour off the water. Repeat once or twice more. Remove and place the sea vegetable into a colander or strainer. Quickly rinse under cold water to remove any heavier dust or particles. The sea vegetables are now ready to be soaked before being sliced.

Washing root or ground vegetables—Vegetables other than leafy greens can be scrubbed with a natural-bristle brush to properly remove soil while keeping the skin intact. Place the vegetables in the sink and run cold water over them. Gently but firmly scrub with the vegetable brush, making sure not to damage the nutrient-rich skin. Green cabbage, most types of lettuce, and Chinese cabbage require removing part or all of the leaves from the core and washing the leaves individually under cold water. Vegetables which have waxed skins require peeling to remove the skin and are then simply rinsed under cold water.

Vegetables such as leeks need to be split lengthwise down the center and each leaf needs to be carefully washed to remove soil. The root portion of leeks, scallions, and chives can be held under cold running water and scrubbed firmly to remove soil between the roots. Vegetables such as burdock have a rather delicate skin that can be easily damaged by scrubbing too firmly. The skin is naturally brown or dark brown in color and is often mistaken for soil. If the skin has turned white when you are finished scrubbing, you have scrubbed too hard.

Cucumbers, if unwaxed, can be washed in the same manner as roots. If waxed, remove the skin, and rinse under cold water before using. For root vegetables with the greens still attached, remove the green portion and wash as you would other leafy greens. The root can be washed as above. Onions can first be peeled and then rinsed quickly under cold water until clean. If vegetables that require peeling are heavily caked with soil, it is a good idea to first scrub the vegetable with the skin left on before peeling and rinsing under cold water. Fresh shiitake and other mushrooms can simply be rinsed thoroughly by hand under cold water, instead of using a vegetable brush.

Washing leafy greens—Before washing greens, sort through them to remove any yellowed or damaged leaves. Next, place the greens in a large bowl or pot and completely cover with cold water. Let them soak for several seconds. Then wash by swishing the leaves around in the water. Remove the leaves and pour off the water. Now take one leaf and wash it thoroughly under cold running water to remove any remaining soil or dust. With tightly curled leaves, such as kale or chard, make sure to gently unfurl them while rinsing to remove any matter hidden from sight. Wash each leaf individually under cold water until completely clean.

Watercress may have small shells in it, so it is important to wash each leaf thoroughly. Celery sometimes has soil caked between the ribs that run up the stalk. To remove it, take a vegetable brush and lightly scrub. Leafy greens such as collards, cabbage, or Chinese cabbage, which have smoother leaves, generally do not require as much effort to wash as vegetables with jagged edges.

Turnip, rutabaga, radish, and daikon tops sometimes have sandy soil attached to them. Rinsing the whole bunch in a pot once or twice is not sufficient to remove the soil. Make sure to rinse each leaf as well under cold water. Some greens, such as lettuce, cabbage, or Chinese cabbage, require removal of the leaves from the core or stem so that each can be washed separately. Broccoli can also be difficult to clean, as it has hundreds of tiny flowerettes tightly packed together. It may require soaking for several minutes before washing and rinsing. Once the greens are thoroughly washed, place them in a colander and allow them to drain before slicing or cooking whole. String beans and peas are very easy to clean and can simply be rinsed individually or in a colander under cold water.

Wild leafy greens and grasses are best if picked in fields that are not close to roads or highways. They can be washed in the same manner as cultivated greens.

It is better not to cut vegetables before you wash them. Once you slice a vegetable, there is more exposed surface area from which nutrients as well as flavor can escape and go into the washing and rinsing water. It is also more difficult to remove soil from cut vegetables than it is from whole ones.

Washing fruits—Most small fruits such as berries can be placed in a pot of cold water and swished around as you would grains. Then remove, place in a colander, and rinse under cold water. Larger fruits such as melons can be scrubbed with a vegetable brush before slicing. Fruits such as apples, pears, peaches, plums, cherries, nectarines, and others can be washed individually under cold water without scrubbing. Dried fruits should be quickly rinsed before soaking and slicing to make sure they are clean. Raisins and currants are exceptions and do not require washing.

Washing other dried foods—Foods such as dried daikon, lotus seeds, and dried lotus root require quick rinsing under cold water before being soaked. Simply place in a bowl, cover with cold water, swish around, and pour off the water. Then place in a colander and quickly rinse under cold water. Dried chestnuts require sorting before being washed and rinsed. Foods such as shiitake mushrooms or dried tofu do not require washing. Roast nuts more evenly if they are quickly rinsed and drained before roasting.

Other Helpful Hints

Some of the whole foods used in this book need to be soaked, puréed, or diluted before being used in cooking. Below are instructions on how to do these basic steps.

Soaking—Dried foods such as beans, sea vegetables, dried chestnuts, lotus seeds, dried lotus root, dried tofu, dried daikon, shiitake mushrooms, and others need to be soaked in order to make them soft enough to cut smoothly. Of course, the amount of time for soaking varies from food to food, but the basic procedure is generally the same. When dried food is called for in one of the recipes in this book, the approximate length of time needed for soaking is included in the recipe. Approximate soaking times are also presented in the table below.

To soak dried foods after washing them, place them in a bowl and add enough cold water to cover. Let the food soak for the length of time indicated in the recipe or in the table before slicing or cooking. Items such as dried tofu and shiitake mushrooms are best soaked in warm rather than cold water.

In most cases the soaking water can be saved and used as part of your water measurement in cooking the foods but there are exceptions. Sea vegetable soaking water, if very salty, can be discarded. Azuki bean and black soybean soaking water can be used in cooking, while the soaking water from beans that are higher in fat is usually discarded. Soaking water from dried daikon, if it is very dark brown, may make a dish taste quite bitter. In this case discard the soaking water. If the dried daikon soaking water is light in color, it is more sweet and is used in cooking. Soaking water from dried tofu is discarded as it has an unpleasant taste. Other soaking waters from items such as fu, shiitake mushrooms, lotus seeds, dried lotus root, and dried chestnuts can be used in cooking.

Food	*Required Soaking Time*
Sea vegetables	3–5 minutes
Dried daikon	5–10 minutes
Dried tofu	5–10 minutes
Fu	7–10 minutes
Dried lotus root	30–60 minutes
Dried lotus seeds	30–60 minutes
Shiitake mushrooms	10–15 minutes
Dried chestnuts	10–15 minutes after roasting
Beans	6–8 hours
Grains	6–8 hours
Dried fruits	15–20 minutes

Diluting—Some dried food items require diluting before adding to recipes. One item which comes up often in macrobiotic cooking is *kuzu* (kudzu). To dilute kuzu, place the correct measurement in a cup or small bowl and add an equal amount or just slightly more cold water to the cup. Stir the kuzu and water to thoroughly dilute and remove lumps. It is now ready to use as a thickener.

Puréeing Miso—Often in this book you will come across recipes requiring puréed miso. Place the correct measurement of miso in a *suribachi*. Add slightly more volume of water than miso to the suribachi. In an even, circular motion, purée the miso with the wooden pestle (*surikogi*), until the miso has a smooth, pastelike consistency. It is now ready to use in salad dressing recipes.

Grinding—To prepare some condiments or dressings you need to grind roasted sea vegetables, seeds, chopped nuts, or other foods in a suribachi. To do this, place the food in a suribachi and grind with the wooden pestle in an even, circular motion. Sea vegetables are usually ground to a fine powder, while seeds and nuts are more lightly ground until half-crushed. If you grind roasted seeds and nuts for a long time they will turn into a thick seed or nut butter, which can also be used in making salad dressings. Large roasted nuts or larger seeds such as pumpkin seeds, usually need to be chopped slightly with a knife before grinding to make this process easier.

Marinating—Often we marinate food items such as vegetables, tofu, fish or seafood in a solution of tamari soy sauce, water, and ginger, or miso, which makes them similar to a quick pickle without the pressure of pressing. To marinate, follow the instructions in the recipe for preparing the marinade, then place the required food item in a bowl. Pour the marinade over the food item, and allow it to sit and absorb the marinade for the length of time indicated in the recipe. The marinated food is now ready to eat or be cooked.

Grating—To finely grate ginger, daikon, or other root vegetables for use in salads, dressings, or garnishes, take a flat grater and set it on a cutting board, table, or other flat surface. Hold it securely with one hand while holding the item to be grated firmly in the other hand. Move the vegetable in a back-and-forth motion over the teeth of the grater until the proper amount is grated. Remove the grated pulp and place in a bowl until ready to use.

Using a Suribachi or Hand Food Mill—The suribachi is useful for grinding food items for use in dressings or condiments. Place the ingredients in the suribachi. Hold the wooden pestle securely with one hand, while holding the suribachi with the other. Grind in an even, circular motion, preferably in one direction, using the grooved sides of the bowl to grind to the desired consistency.

A hand food mill can also be used to purée items such as tofu, soft-cooked vegetables, fruits, or grains, and can be used in preparing dressings. Simply set the food mill on top of a bowl so that it fits securely and place the food item in the mill. Hold the mill handle with one hand and turn the hand grinder with the other until the food is smooth and is squeezed through the little holes in the mill. Allow the ground food to fall into the bowl underneath the mill. The food is now ready to use in preparing dressings, sauces, or dips.

Roasting—Items such as seeds, nuts, grains or sea vegetables can be oven-roasted or pan-roasted on top of the stove. Oven-roasting is used most often when preparing sea vegetable condiments. Simply place the unwashed sea vegetable (kombu, wakame, dulse, kelp) on a dry baking or cookie sheet. Place in a 350°F. oven for about 15 to 20 minutes or until crisp but not burnt or black. Remove and grind in a suribachi. Seeds, dried chestnuts, grains, and nuts often roast more evenly when placed in a dry skillet on top of the stove. First wash or rinse the item to be roasted and then allow it to drain. Next, place the damp item in a skillet over a high flame. Take a bamboo rice paddle, and using a back-and-forth motion, quickly but gently move the food back and forth to evenly roast. When the water has evaporated, reduce the flame to medium and continue roasting until golden. Often seeds and grains will begin to pop when they are done and release a nutty fragrance.

You may occasionally shake the skillet gently back and forth to bring seeds from the bottom to the top, thus roasting more evenly. When done remove immediately.

Chapter 4

The Art of Garnishing

Garnishing your dishes properly is an important aspect of macrobiotic cooking. The right garnish helps to balance the energies in foods. For example, soba noodles have more contracting energy. When served by themselves or with a few drops of tamari soy sauce or light tamari broth, their energy can be a little one-sided. However, garnishing each bowl of noodles with freshly cut scallions (which have strong upward energy) transforms them into a masterpiece of yin and yang balance. Similarly, fish or seafood are incomplete without the proper garnish, especially grated raw daikon, which helps the body digest fats and oils.

Similarly, the use of garnishes and fancy, attractive cutting techniques transforms salad making into an art. Garnishes add color and beauty, stimulate the appetite, and harmonize the tastes, colors, and energies of the ingredients. Most garnishes require little energy and time to prepare, and usually no special utensils other than a sharp vegetable or paring knife. Simple garnishes are often enough for salads served at home, while for special occasions, fancier garnishes are sometimes nice. Some of the garnishes used in macrobiotic salad making include:

Sprigs of parsley or watercress	Lemon, lime, or tangerine slices, wedges, or twists
Sliced scallions, chives, or parsley	
Roasted seeds	Pine needles
Roasted and chopped nuts	Clean leaves
Green nori flakes	Flowers
Powdered sea-vegetable condiments	Raisins
Croutons (deep-fried or dry-roasted)	Cooked, thinly sliced shiitake mushrooms
Sliced red-radish rounds	
Lemon rind	Marinated tofu cubes
Tangerine rind	Tofu-cheese cubes
Grated daikon	Fancy vegetable and fruit garnishes
Grated ginger root	Sprouts
Toasted nori squares or strips	Whole lettuce leaves
Grated horseradish or wasabi	Bonito (shaved dried fish) flakes

Please note that these garnishes are fine for use by persons in generally good health. Those with serious illnesses may omit any of the above ingredients until their condition improves. Now let us see how to make some of the more unfamiliar garnishes listed above.

Toasted Nori Strips or Squares—Toasted nori is often used as a garnish for salads. To toast or roast the nori, hold the sheet over the flame on a gas burner so that the shiny, smooth side faces up. Hold the nori about 10 to 12 inches above the flame, and rotate it over the flame until the color changes from dark green or black-purple to a light green. This will take only a few seconds.

Once the nori is toasted, fold the sheet in half and tear or cut along the fold with a pair of scissors. Then fold in half again and tear or cut. You now have four equal-sized squares. Stack the squares on top of each other and cut them into strips 1 to 2 inches wide. Next, cut the strips into 1-inch squares or thin, match-stick-style strips. The nori is now ready to use as a garnish.

Sprouts—Although sprouts can be purchased prepackaged in most natural food stores, it is often nice to use freshly made sprouts rather than those that are several days old. The older the sprouts are the more bitter their flavor becomes. Before making sprouts, make sure that the seeds you have purchased are natural, organic, and untreated. The most common seeds or beans used for sprouting are alfalfa seeds, yellow soybeans, mung beans, and daikon radish seeds made especially for sprouting. Many types of beans and some seeds can be toxic, especially if eaten in large quantities. To make sure that the seeds you wish to sprout are not harmful, it is a good idea to purchase a book on sprouting for reference.

To begin the sprouting process, first wash the seeds or beans as described in Chapter 3. Then place them in a bowl or large glass jar. Cover them with fresh cold water and let them soak overnight. Then, remove the soaking water and discard. Rinse the seeds or beans under cold water and place them in a clean glass jar or sprouting container. Cover the jar or container with clean cotton cheesecloth or the lid of a jar made from wire mesh to allow air circulation. Place the jar in a warm cupboard or on a shaded windowsill. Next, rinse the seeds with cold water twice per day—morning and evening. If the seeds are not rinsed regularly, they may turn sour or become moldy. Sprouts are ready when they reach the following lengths: alfalfa, 1 to 2 inches; mung beans, 1 to 3 inches; yellow soybeans, 2 to 3 inches; daikon radish sprouts, 1 to 1 1/2 inches.

The sprouts are now ready to use. Alfalfa and daikon radish sprouts are usually served raw in salads. Mung bean sprouts may be eaten raw, boiled, or sautéed. Soybean sprouts are a little difficult to digest in their raw form, and are usually boiled, steamed, or sautéed before eating.

Once your sprouts are ready, put them in the refrigerator to keep them fresh and to prevent souring.

There are many ways to sprout seeds and beans, using special sprouting kits, jars, or a sprouting base. Also, sprouting in darkness produces a whiter, crispier sprout while sprouting in a light but shaded area produces a softer texture and greener sprout. There are many books available on the subject for further information.

Croutons—Croutons are nice for occasional use on simple or mixed salads. As described below, they can be dry-roasted, oven-roasted, or deep-fried.

- *Dry-roasting*—Dice fresh or slightly dried whole wheat, sourdough, or rice bread. Place a dry skillet on a medium flame and heat up. Place the diced bread in the skillet and dry-roast until golden brown, stirring constantly to evenly toast and prevent burning. When dry, sprinkle with a few drops of tamari soy sauce, if desired, and roast another minute or so. If you do not wish to season the cubes with tamari soy sauce, omit it. The croutons are now ready to use.

Persons who do not have to watch their oil intake may occasionally roast the diced cubes in a small amount of light or dark sesame or corn oil instead of dry-roasting them.

- *Oven-roasting*—Dice bread as above and place on a baking sheet. Place in a 350°F. oven and dry-roast, stirring occasionally to evenly roast, until completely dried out and golden brown. Season with a small amount of tamari soy sauce as above, mix, and dry-roast several more minutes until completely dry.

- *Deep-frying*—Dice the bread as above, and drop into hot, light or dark sesame oil. Deep-fry until golden brown. Drain on paper towels to remove excess oil. The croutons are now ready to use.

Roasted Sesame Seeds (Tan or Black)—Wash a small amount (1/8 to 1/4 cup) of sesame seeds as instructed in the previous chapter. Place in a fine-mesh strainer and allow them to drain for several minutes. Heat a stainless-steel skillet and place the damp seeds in it. Set the flame to medium. Dry-roast, stirring or moving the seeds back and forth with a rice paddle until they begin to pop. When the seeds release a nutty fragrance, turn color (tan seeds turn slightly golden, black seeds become lighter in color), and can be easily crushed when held between the little finger and thumb, they are done. The seeds are now ready to use as a garnish or to prepare dressings or condiments.

Roasted Sunflower and Pumpkin Seeds—Wash, drain, and dry-roast these seeds as you would sesame seeds. Pumpkin seeds are done when they begin to pop and turn slightly brown. Sunflower seeds do not pop but are done when they turn golden in color. You may use the seeds as is for garnishes, or in preparing dressings. You may also season them with a few drops of tamari soy sauce at the very end of cooking for a slightly salty flavor. When you do this, roast the seeds for several more seconds until the tamari soy sauce dries on them.

Roasted Nuts—Place shelled nuts in a hot skillet and dry-roast or place on a baking sheet and oven-roast. Stir occasionally to evenly roast and prevent burning. You may season with several drops of tamari soy sauce at the end of cooking or remove and use unseasoned (either whole or chopped) as a garnish or in salad dressings.

As a variation, first blanch the nuts by pouring boiling water over them and allowing them to sit for 1 to 2 minutes. Then dry-roast in an oven or skillet. This helps the nuts roast more thoroughly and evenly.

Try not to roast the nuts until they become scorched or burnt, as this causes them to have a bitter flavor.

As a variation, which is especially nice for almonds, boil the nuts for 1 to 2 minutes, drain, and remove the skins by squeezing them slightly. Then slice, sliver, or dry-roast as above.

Chopped Nuts or Seeds—Roast the nuts or seeds as above, then place them in a circular mound on a cutting board. Hold the knife with the tip on the board. Using a circular, rocking motion, move the blade from the tip to the hilt or opposite end, gradually cutting or working in a half-circle, until all the nuts or seeds are chopped. If larger pieces are desired, such as when walnuts or pecans are used, simply break them into the desired size with your fingers.

Minced Vegetables—Mincing is simply a method of chopping vegetables very finely. Minced scallions, parsley, chives, onions, or carrot tops can be used often in salad dressings. Minced vegetables are often much more flavorful than larger slices, especially in salad dressings. Simply place the vegetable on a cutting board and chop into very small pieces.

Grated Vegetables or Fruits—Sometimes vegetables or fruits can be finely grated and used to garnish salads or in preparing dressings. Please refer to Chapter 3 for instructions on using a grater.

Marinated Tofu—Drain a cake of tofu, and slice into bite-sized cubes. Place in a bowl and sprinkle with several drops of tamari soy sauce or umeboshi vinegar, gently mix, and let sit for 30 minutes or so. Remove, drain, and use to garnish salads.

As a variation, you may prepare a marinade by combining a small amount of water, tamari soy sauce or umeboshi vinegar, and a dab of grated ginger. Mix the marinade and pour it over the tofu. Gently mix and allow to marinate 30 minutes or so.

Tofu Cheese—A slightly fermented flavor is sometimes nice in salads, and this can be achieved by adding tofu cheese. Tofu cheese is made by coating whole or halved cakes of tofu with barley miso, umeboshi vinegar and water, or tamari soy sauce and water, and allowing it to sit for 3 to 4 days.

To make tofu cheese with miso, take a cake of very fresh tofu, and drain it for several minutes. Wrap a layer of clean cotton cheesecloth around the tofu cake. Pack barley miso all around the covered tofu cake until it is completely covered with miso. Place in a bowl or ceramic crock. Cover the crock or bowl with a piece of cheesecloth, and let it sit for 2 to 4 days. For mild-tasting tofu cheese, let it sit for 2 days, and for a stronger flavor, let it sit for 3 to 4 days.

When finished, remove the miso-coated cheesecloth from the tofu cake. Rinse the tofu under cold water. Slice into cubes for use as a garnish, or into larger slices which can be served with crackers or bread. Tofu cheese can be puréed in a suribachi or hand food mill to make a dip for crudités.

The miso can be removed from the cheesecloth and saved to be used again, or to season soups, although it will have a milder flavor, as the tofu absorbs much of the salt it contains.

These are just a few of the many natural foods that can be used to garnish and enhance the flavor and beauty of your salads. Feel free to experiment and discover new and wonderful garnishes to make your salads flavorful and exciting.

Basic Cutting

In this section we introduce a variety of ways to cut vegetables for use in salads and other dishes, and in making garnishes. Below are basic vegetable cutting techniques that are used most frequently. Choosing the right cuts for your salad vegetables is very important both in terms of flavor and appearance. In macrobiotic cooking we often cut vegetables on an angle, which makes it possible to create a large variety of beautiful cuts. However, at times we also cut them straight across, as we do with cuts such as rounds, rectangles, and diced vegetables.

When several styles of cutting are combined in one dish, it is better to keep the cuts generally the same in terms of size and thickness. Also, when you cut vegetables into large chunks, it is better to keep them bite-sized so that it is easier to eat them. With continual practice, your knife technique and speed of cutting will improve, so do not be overwhelmed if vegetable cutting seems difficult at first.

The proper use of your knife is essential in smooth and effortless cutting. Grip the knife handle firmly with either hand. If you are right-handed, curl your index, middle, ring, and little fingers firmly around the right side of the handle. Rest your thumb firmly against the left side of the handle. Grip firmly with all of your fingers, but not too tightly. Holding your knife too tightly can make your arm tire quickly, especially if you have a lot of cutting to do. It can also interfere with your ability

Hand Positions and Vegetable Chopping

to make smooth, clean cuts. Actually, the thumb and index finger can be used to apply the most pressure. The other fingers can be used to balance the handle, thus making knife control easier.

When holding the vegetables that are being cut, curl your fingers in slightly at the first joint. This prevents or reduces the chance of cutting yourself while slicing. Tilt the blade slightly away from your fingers, with the upper portion of the blade resting gently against the middle or end joint of your middle finger. Place the blade on the vegetable and slide it firmly but gently forward through the vegetable, with a slight downward pressure.

Cut with the entire length of the blade. It is best not to saw or push down too hard to the extent that the knife tears through the vegetable. This produces jagged slices that are not so attractive or harmonious in terms of their energy balance.

Sometimes, when slicing long vegetables or leafy greens, we use a cutting technique known as the "drawing motion." In this method, we use only the tip of the knife. Place the tip on the vegetable and draw the blade back toward you until the entire length of it is cut.

The most commonly used methods for cutting vegetables are presented in the diagram below.

Vegetable Cutting Styles

Fancy Cutting ————————————————

In addition to the basic cutting methods described above, more fancy techniques are sometimes appropriate when preparing garnishes, especially for special occasions. Fancy garnishes enhance the beauty of the salads, aspics, or kantens you prepare. Vegetables can be cut into shapes that resemble roses and other flowers, fans, baskets, brushes, chains, springs, loops, curls, twigs, pine needles, combs, birds, trees, mushrooms, butterflies, fishnets, and so on. These colorful garnishes are quick and simple to prepare, and can be used for any occasion.

Carrot or Radish Curls

Cut a carrot or small daikon radish into 3-inch sections. Only 1 to 2 sections are needed. Peel the skin with a vegetable peeler. Then, with a Japanese vegetable knife, peel a thin sheet from the carrot by turning the carrot into the blade. Slowly peel by applying gentle pressure with your left thumb. Try to make the thin sheet of carrot or daikon as long as possible.

Next, lay the thin vegetable sheet flat on the cutting board and cut it on a diagonal into strips that are 1/8 to 1/4 inch wide. Place the strips in very cold water, which will cause them to curl. When the strips curl completely, remove and use.

Vegetable Curls

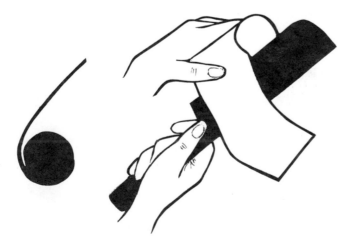

Carrot or Radish Curls

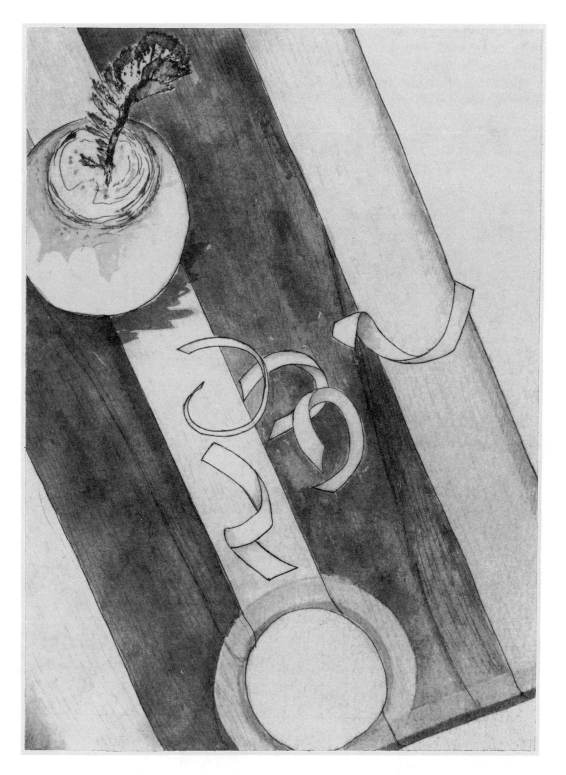

Carrot Flowers

Cut a 3-inch-long section of carrot. Stand the carrot section on end and trim the sides to produce a five-sided pentagon shape. With a Japanese vegetable knife, make five shallow, lengthwise cuts in the carrot section as shown. Shape one end of the carrot section so that it looks like a pencil. Then slice the flowers from the section as shown.

Carrot Flowers

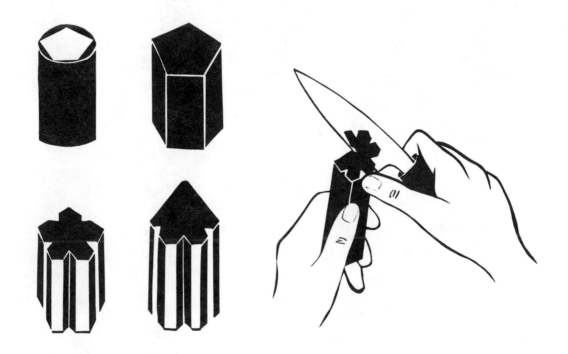

Carrot Flowers

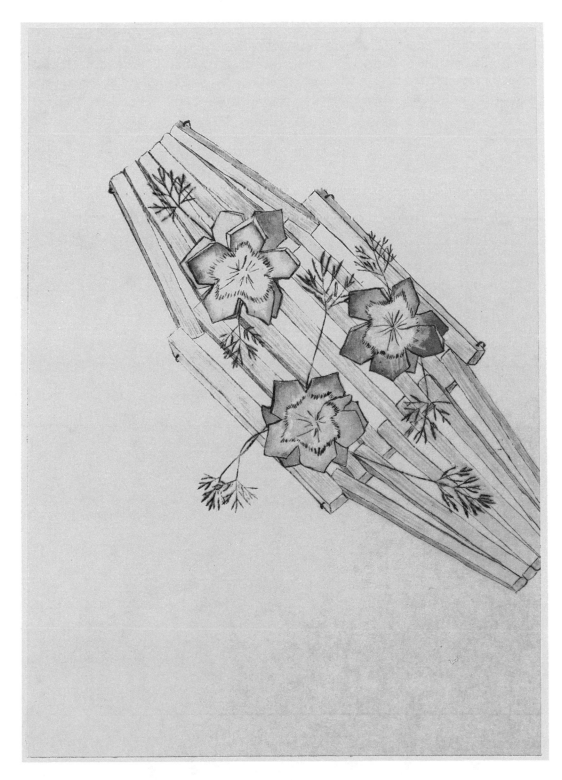

Carrot Maple Leaves

Trim the ends from a fairly thick carrot. Cut the carrot into a 1-inch-thick cylinder or round shape. Stand the cylinder on end and trim off the sides so that you have a five-sided pentagon shape. With a paring or serrated knife, cut the carrot into the shape of a maple leaf. When finished, cut little notches in the edges of the leaves, and then slice into individual leaves.

Carrot Maple Leaf

Carrot Maple Leaves

Julienne-style Vegetable Bundles

These bundles can be made with carrots, daikon, rutabaga, green and yellow string beans, parsnips, snow peas, celery, and turnips. Slice the vegetables into 2 1/2- to 3-inch lengths. Next, slice in thin matchsticks or julienne strips.

Place a small amount of water in a saucepan and bring to a boil. Place the vegetables in the boiling water and blanch for several seconds to 1 minute. Remove, drain, and run under cold water to set the color. Stack the vegetables into several small bundles and tie them together with thin strips of cooked scallion, leeks, kombu, or cooked gourd strips. They are now ready to use as a garnish.

Julienne Vegetable Bundles

Julienne-style Vegetable Bundles

Cucumber Fans

Take an unwaxed, unpeeled cucumber and trim off the ends. Next, slice the cucumber in half lengthwise. Make a row of very thin (1/8 inch thick) slices down the entire length of the cucumber, leaving a 1/4-inch-thick spine along the opposite side to hold the cucumber slices together. Place the cucumber in a bowl of cold water with about 1 tablespoon of sea salt diluted in it, making sure the cucumber is completely covered. Let sit for 10 to 15 minutes. Remove and rinse under cold water. Make a flower or leaf shape out of a carrot. Place the cucumber fan on a plate and spread it out so that it circles about 1/3 of the edge of the plate, and resembles a fan. Place the carrot flower or leaf at one end of the cucumber fan. The plate is now ready to have the salad arranged on it.

Cucumber Fan

Cucumber Twists

Cucumber Twists

Take a long cucumber with few seeds and slice about 1/3 of the cucumber length-wise from the sides. Place the thin slice on a cutting board with the flat side facing down. Slice one end off on a diagonal or 30-degree angle. Make a series of diagonal slices that are about 1/8 inch thick down the entire length of the cucumber, leaving a 1/4-inch-thick spine along the opposite edge to hold the cucumber together. Place the cucumber in a bowl of water with about 1 tablespoon of sea salt diluted in it, and let sit for 10 to 15 minutes. Remove and rinse. Place on a cutting board and fold every other slice in toward the cucumber. Place on a serving plate and arrange your salad around the cucumber twist garnish.

Cucumber Twists

Daikon Curls

Celery, Daikon, or Turnip Curls

Cut the leaves from a turnip, daikon, or stalk of celery. Cut the leaf away from the hard stem. Make a series of angular shallow slits down the entire length of the stem. Then cut the stem lengthwise into three thin strips. Drop the strips into cold water and let sit until curled tightly. Remove and use as garnish.

Daikon Curls

Lemon, Lime, Tangerine, or Cucumber Baskets

Select a nicely shaped lemon without discoloration. Make a slice slightly off center about halfway through the lemon. Cut another slice about 1/4 inch away from the previous cut to the same depth, leaving a piece in the center of the lemon to serve as the handle for the basket. Make a horizontal slice from the end of the lemon in toward the handle and lift the wedge out. Repeat at the other end of the lemon.

The lemon should now start to resemble a basket. Use a paring knife to cut the inside of the lemon away from underneath the handle. Next, with a knife or melon baller, remove the inside of the lemon from the base of the basket. The basket can now be filled with parsley or watercress sprigs, celery leaves, thin carrot curls, or other items. Arrange your salad on a serving platter or bowl and garnish with the lemon basket.

Lemon Basket

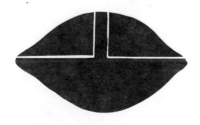

Lemon Baskets

Lemon, Lime, or Tangerine Butteflies

Choose a firm lemon, lime, or tangerine and cut into several thin rounds. Remove the seeds. Cut a V-shaped wedge from one side of the lemon slice. Turn the slice around and cut another wedge directly across from the previous one. Take a carrot, daikon, parsnip, or other colorful vegetable and cut two very thin strips or matchsticks to use for antennae. Place your salad on a platter and arrange the butterfly garnish. This garnish is also very lovely on top of an aspic or kanten.

Lemon Butterflies

Lemon Butterflies

Cucumber Boats

Trim the ends from a cucumber and discard. Slice the cucumber into 2- to 3-inch-long sections. Cut each section in half. In each half section, make a thin lengthwise slice which is parallel to the center of the cucumber, leaving about 1/4 inch at the end of the section attached or unsliced. Curl or fold back the slice and stick a toothpick through it to secure it to the cucumber base. Scoop the seeds out to form a hollow chamber in the boat.

The cucumber sections should now resemble a small sailboat. Fill the chamber with tofu dip, tofu cheese, hummus, or seafood salad. These can be used as dips for crudités or as spreads for crackers and bread wedges. Arrange the crudités, crackers or bread on a platter and garnish the platter with several stuffed cucumber boats.

Cucumber Boat

Cucumber Boat

Lemon Twist

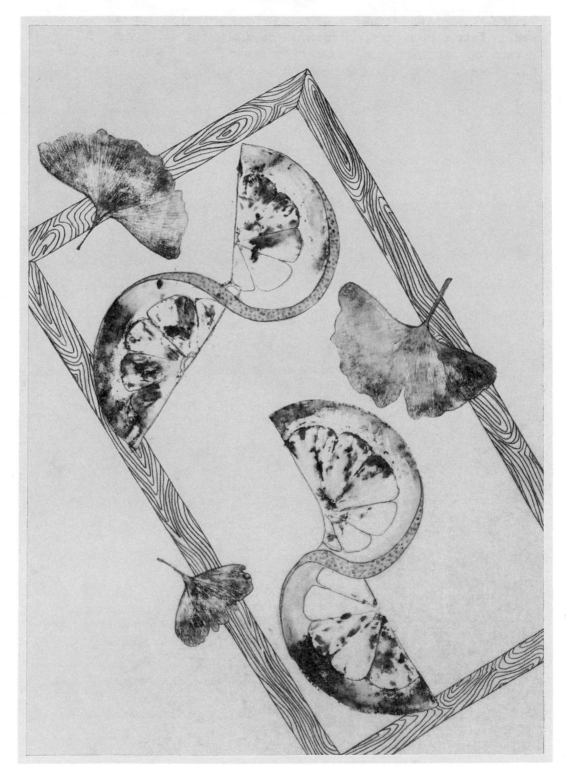

Lemon, Lime, or Tangerine Twists

These take only a few seconds to prepare and can be used for any salad, aspic or kanten. Take a lemon, lime, or tangerine and slice it into thin rounds. Make a slice in each round, stopping at the center of the round. Next, twist the slice so the ends face in opposite directions. The twists are now ready to use.

Lemon Twists

Turnip or Red Radish Chrysanthemums

Take a medium-sized, purple-topped or white turnip, or a large red radish and remove the stem and root portions. You may peel the vegetable or leave the colorful skin on. Next, place the vegetable on a cutting board between two chopsticks. Make a series of thin slices that run down the entire vegetable. The chopsticks prevent the knife from slicing all the way through the vegetable, leaving a base to hold the slices together. Now, turn the vegetable around 90 degrees and make another series of slices at right angles to the previous slices.

Dilute about a tablespoon of sea salt in a bowl of water and place the turnip or radish in it so that it is completely covered. Let it sit for 10 to 15 minutes, or until the turnip or radish completely opens up. Remove and rinse under cold water. For additional color, you may add a few drops of umeboshi vinegar on top of the chrysanthemums for a soft pink color. Arrange your salad on a platter or in a bowl. Set the chrysanthemum on the side or in the center of the salad. Pick two or three leaves from a small rose bush or other plant and wash. Arrange the leaves under the chrysanthemum to resemble a flower with leaves.

Turnip or Red Radish Mums

Turnip Chrysanthemum

Melon Fans

Melon Fans

Slice a cantaloupe or small honeydew melon into 1/2-inch-thick rounds. Cut each round into thirds. Remove the seeds and a small amount of the inside of the melon from the center of the slices with a curved object such as a small metal measuring spoon or paring knife. Peel the skin from each slice. You should now have a semicircle or fan-shape slice. Now, make five slanted cuts on the front of the melon slices about 1/4-inch deep, and remove the wedges. The melon fans are now ready to be used as garnish.

Melon Fan

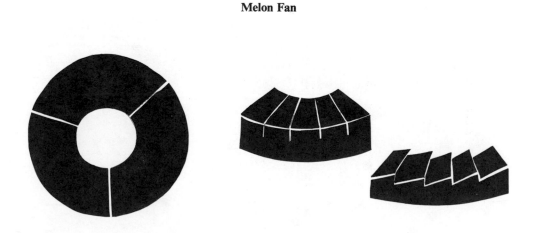

Scallion Whisks

Scallion Whisks

Take a scallion and remove the roots. Cut about a 3-inch section from the scallion. The bottom part of each section is comprised of the white part of the scallion and a small amount of the top part of the section will be green. Slice the scallion into many very thin slivers, rolling or rotating it to make as many slices as possible. Leave a 1/2-inch section of the white part of the scallion unsliced to serve as a base to hold the whisk together (you may refer to this as the "handle"). Place the sliced scallion in very cold water until it is completely curled and resembles a whisk or brush. Remove and use as garnish.

Scallion Whisk

Lotus Flowers

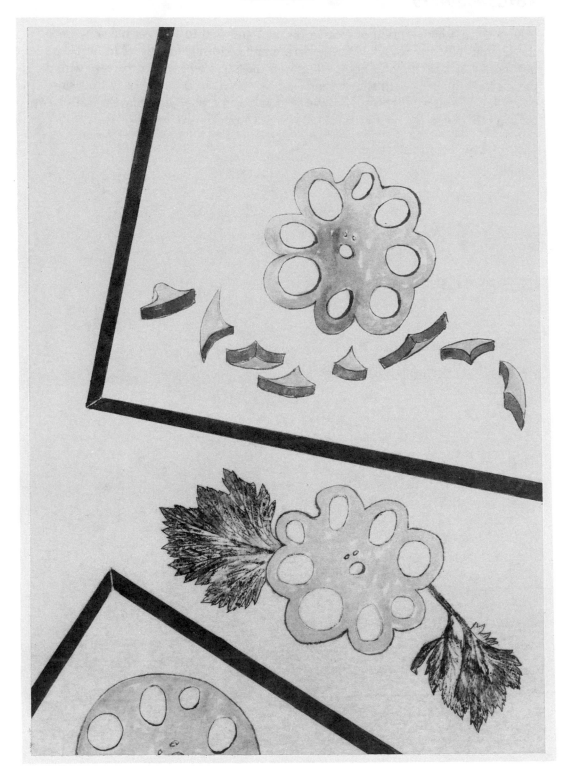

Lotus Flowers

Take a 3- to 4-inch section of fresh lotus root and peel to remove the skin. Slice the section into thin rounds. With a paring knife, cut out the pieces in between the natural pattern of the lotus root. Round off the edges wherever necessary with a paring knife, so that each slice resembles a flower. Take a few parsley leaves or celery leaves and wash them. Arrange your salad in a bowl and place a leaf or two on top of it. Set a slice of lotus root flower on top of the leaves.

Red Radish Tops

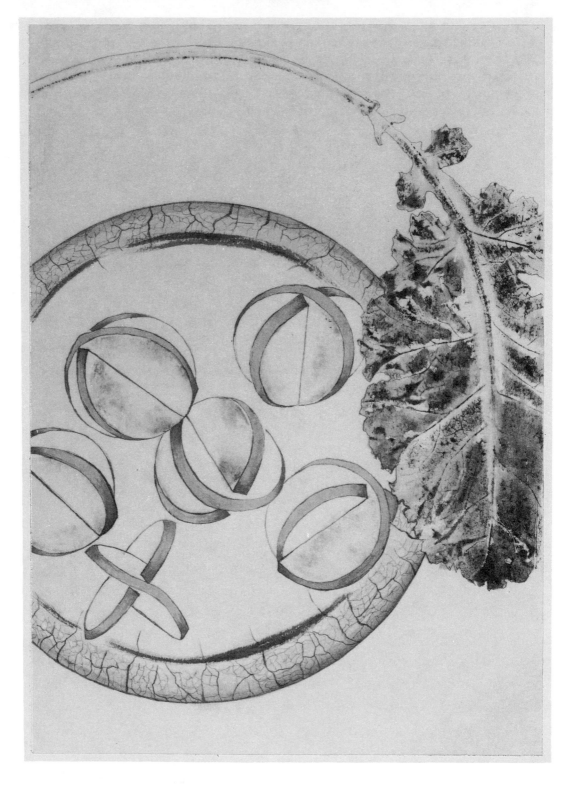

Red Radish Tops

All you need to make these are radishes and a paring knife. You can make several in just a minute or so. Remove the top stem and the root from the radish. Then slice the radish into several 1/8-inch-thick rounds. Make a notch in each slice of radish only to the center of each slice. Hold one radish slice in each hand and gently slide one slice into the other at the notch to connect them. Repeat until several are made. They are now ready to garnish any salad.

Red Radish Tops

 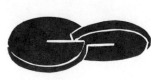 

Red Radish Flowers

For this lovely garnish you will need fresh red radishes with the greens still attached. Wash and remove the root portion of the radish. Slice the radish root into very thin (1/8 to 1/16 inch thick) slices. Place the root portion in a bowl of water with about 1 tablespoon of sea salt dissolved in it. Let it sit for 10 to 15 minutes. Do not place the leaf section in the salt solution. Remove and rinse. Place your salad in a serving dish and set the radish flower off to the side or in the center of it. Spread the radish part open slightly with your fingers to resemble a flower or fan shape.

Red Radish Flowers

Vegetable Twists

Take vegetables such as carrots, summer squash, or daikon and slice into thin rectangular shapes about 1/8 inch thick. Make a 1-inch slit in the center of each rectangle. Place the slices in a bowl of water with 1 tablespoon of sea salt diluted in it and let sit for 10 to 15 minutes. Remove the slices and rinse. Next, slip one end of each slice through the 1-inch notch in the center and pull back, creating a twisted shape. The vegetables are now ready to garnish your salad.

Vegetable Twists

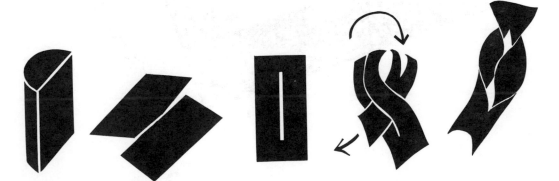

Vegetable Twists

Condiments, Dressings, and Dips

Although macrobiotic salads are delicious as is, condiments and dressings can make them even more enjoyable. Condiments are an excellent way to add minerals and other nutrients to foods, and when made with roasted seeds, they provide a balanced source of natural oils. Condiments can also make foods easier to digest.

The condiments presented below are delicious when lightly sprinkled on grain, noodle, cooked-vegetable, and raw salads. They can be used in place of dressings. Keep several varieties on your table at all times so that each person can sprinkle or add them to salads and other dishes as they like. These condiments are all delicious, so be careful not to overuse them. A pinch now and then is usually sufficient. Also, if you make condiments for children, reduce the amount of salt or ground sea-vegetable powders called for in the recipes. Children require much less salt than adults, and babies do not require any. Please refer to our cookbook for children, *Macrobiotic Family Favorites* (Japan Publications, Inc.), for specific recipes.

Below are a few of the many condiments that can be prepared for use on salads. Additional recipes can be found in cookbooks listed in the bibliography. Also, feel free to experiment and create new ones.

Condiments ———————————————

Gomashio (Sesame Salt)

A salty and slightly bitter-tasting condiment, that gives a delicious nutty flavor to foods, gomashio can be sprinkled on grain, noodle, cooked-vegetable, and raw-vegetable salads.

Gomashio can be bought prepackaged in natural and macrobiotic food stores, but as with other prepared foods, fresh, homemade gomashio is far better. Fresh gomashio can be made about once a week. The word *gomashio* comes from *goma*, or "sesame," and *shio*, or "salt."

Either variety of sesame seed—tan or black can be used to prepare gomashio. Tan seeds are less bitter and contain more oil, while black ones are a little more bitter but contain less oil. Gomashio is an excellent, balanced source of whole oil and minerals. The sea salt used in gomashio aids in the digestion of the natural oil in the seeds: the more yang elements in sea salt provide a counterbalance to the yin elements in the sesame oil.

The standard proportion of sea salt to sesame seeds in adult gomashio is about from 1 to 14 to 16. For children, use much less salt or none at all.

Patience is the key to making delicious gomashio. It is better not to prepare it too hastily. To store gomashio, allow it to cool completely, place it in a tightly sealed glass jar, and store in a cupboard.

> **1 cup sesame seeds (tan or black), washed and drained**
> **1–1⅓ Tbsp. sea salt**

Place the sea salt in a skillet and dry-roast 2 to 3 minutes, stirring constantly. Remove and place in a suribachi. Grind to a fine powder.

Take another skillet and heat on a medium flame. Add the drained sesame seeds. Stir with a constant back-and-forth motion with a rice paddle, shaking the skillet from time to time so that the seeds roast evenly and do not burn. Burnt seeds give gomashio a very bitter flavor. When the seeds give off a nutty fragrance, darken in color, and begin popping, take a seed and hold it between your thumb and little finger. If it crushes easily, the seeds are done. If not, roast a little longer.

As soon as the seeds are done, immediately pour them into the suribachi. If the seeds are left in the hot skillet for even a few seconds after roasting, they will burn. Add the sea salt and, with a wooden pestle (surikogi), slowly grind the seeds and salt with an even, circular motion. Grind until the seeds are about completely crushed. Do not hurry. Allow the gomashio to cool before storing.

Sea-vegetable and Sesame-sea-vegetable Sprinkles

Sea vegetable sprinkles are an excellent source of minerals. They can be prepared simply by themselves or combined with roasted sesame seeds.

To prepare plain sea-vegetable sprinkles, take unwashed wakame, kombu, kelp, or dulse and place it on a baking sheet. Place in a 350°F. oven and dry-roast until

---

Note: In the recipes, Tbsp. refers to tablespoon and tsp. refers to teaspoon.

the sea vegetable becomes crisp and crumbles easily. This will take about 15 to 20 minutes. Be careful not to roast the sea vegetable too long, as this will cause it to burn and turn black, producing a bitter-tasting condiment. After roasting, remove, place in a suribachi, and grind to a fine powder. Sprinkle on any grain, noodle, or cooked-vegetable salad.

To prepare sesame-sea-vegetable sprinkles, roast the sea vegetables (wakame, kombu, kelp, or dulse) as described above. Then roast tan sesame seeds as you would if making gomashio. The general proportion can be about 60 percent sesame seeds to about 40 percent sea vegetable. First place the roasted sea vegetable in a suribachi and grind to a fine powder. Then add the roasted sesame seeds and grind until half-crushed. Allow to cool completely before storing. Make fresh about once per week.

Shiso-leaf Condiments

Shiso leaves are the dark red or purplish-colored leaves that come with the umeboshi plums that you purchase. Shiso leaves give the plums their red color.

There are two types of shiso leaves—red and green. The pickled red leaves are used for making condiments, quick pickles, garnishes, or for seasoning salad dressings and other foods. Freshly picked green leaves can be purchased in season, and are often used as a garnish with sushi or grain salads, and as seasoning in sushi. The English word for shiso is "beefsteak plant."

Red shiso leaves can be purchased in three forms: in with umeboshi plums; as large, fancy, whole leaves, prepackaged; and as a dried, prepackaged condiment. The shiso that comes with umeboshi plums or the pickled whole leaves can be chopped or finely minced, and mixed with grain, noodle, or vegetable salads and aspics. A small quantity of shiso is sufficient. The dried, condiment variety can also be used as above; sprinkled on salads; or combined with other items to prepare other condiments and dressings.

Sesame-Shiso Condiment

> ½ cup roasted tan sesame seeds
> 2 Tbsp. dried shiso-leaf condiment

Place the roasted sesame seeds in a suribachi and grind until about crushed. Add the shiso leaves and grind lightly to mix. Use as a sprinkle on salads or other dishes.

Green Nori Flake Condiment (Aonori)

This is a different species of nori than that used in sheet nori. Nori flakes are a good source of iron and are not salty. They add an appetizing flavor to salads or other dishes, and can be used in dressings. These flakes are fine for children because of their low salt content.

Green nori flakes can be purchased prepackaged in macrobiotic and natural food stores. Sprinkle on grain, noodle, or vegetable salads.

Green Nori Flake-Shiso-Sesame Condiment

> 2 Tbsp. green nori flakes
> 2 tsp. dried shiso leaves
> 1/4 cup roasted tan or black sesame seeds

Place the shiso leaves in a suribachi and grind to a fine powder. Add the sesame seeds, and grind until crushed. Add the nori flakes and simply mix them in. Sprinkle on a variety of salads and other dishes.

Other Condiments

As we have mentioned, there are hundreds of other condiments or variations of the above that you can prepare for different occasions. The following condiments add a rich flavor to salads.

Pumpkin or Sunflower-seed Condiment

> 1 cup pumpkin or sunflower seeds, washed, dry-roasted, and seasoned with
>   a few drops of tamari soy sauce (refer to the previous chapter for
>   roasting instructions)

After roasting and seasoning the pumpkin or sunflower seeds, place them on a cutting board. Chop coarsely. Place in a suribachi and grind to a coarse consistency. Sprinkle on any grain, noodle, or vegetable salad.

Carrot-top and Sesame Condiment

> 1 bunch fresh carrot tops, washed
> 1/2 cup roasted sesame seeds
> Tamari soy sauce

Mince the carrot tops. Place enough water in a skillet just to lightly cover the bottom. Bring to a boil. Add the carrot tops, cover, and steam 1 minute or until bright green. Remove.

Place the roasted sesame seeds in a suribachi and grind until crushed. Add the carrot tops to the suribachi and mix thoroughly with the sesame seeds. Sprinkle a few drops of tamari soy sauce on the mixture, for a mild salt flavor, and mix again.

Sprinkle on any grain, noodle, or cooked-vegetable salad.

Parsley and Sesame Condiment

> 1 bunch fresh parsley, washed
> 1/2 cup roasted sesame seeds
> Tamari soy sauce

Prepare as you would carrot-top and sesame-seed condiment. As a variation, instead of using roasted sesame seeds in the above recipes, try using roasted, chopped pumpkin or sunflower seeds for a different flavor.

Dressings

When you decide to serve your salad with a dressing, choosing the right one is essential. A dressing can either enhance your salad and make it even more delicious, or diminish its flavor and disturb the harmony of the ingredients. Ideally, a dressing should complement the ingredients and bring forth the natural flavor of the salad. Balancing your salad with the appropriate dressing is an art that requires sensitivity and imagination.

Salads dressings can stimulate any of the five tastes—salty, sour, pungent, sweet, and bitter. These flavors can be supplied by using the following ingredients:

Salty—by using tamari soy sauce, sea salt, or miso as a base for the dressing

Sour—by using items such as umeboshi plums and paste, umeboshi vinegar, brown rice vinegar, sweet brown rice vinegar, hato mugi vinegar, apple cider vinegar, or tangerine, orange, lemon, or lime juice

Pungent—by using items such as fresh ginger or its juice, grated daikon, scallions, chives, horseradish, or wasabi

Sweet—by using miso, mirin, apple juice, grated fruit, barley malt, rice syrup, raisins, or sweet vegetables

Bitter—by using roasted seeds and nuts, sea vegetable flakes or powders, tahini, sesame butter, parsley, or watercress

Quality Ingredients

When preparing dressings, it is important to select the highest quality natural ingredients, in order to achieve the fullest flavor, and for the salad and dressing to be beneficial for health. Dressings that contain sugar, animal fat, tropical spices, honey, or chemical additives are not recommended. Many of the high-quality seasonings listed in Chapter 2 can be used in salad dressings by persons in good health.

How to Prepare Kombu Dashi (Broth)

Kombu broth, or *dashi*, can be used as a base for dressings and marinades. To prepare, wipe a 4- to 6-inch piece of kombu with a clean, damp sponge. Place 3 to 4 cups of water in a saucepan and add the kombu. Bring almost to a boil. Reduce the flame to medium-low, and simmer 4 to 5 minutes. Remove the kombu and save for use in other dishes. The broth is now ready for use in making salad dressings.

Occasionally, dried bonito flakes can be added to the dashi for additional flavor. Add the flakes after you remove the kombu, and simmer for another 7 to 10 minutes. Strain the dashi to remove the bonito flakes. The broth is now ready to use.

If storing kombu dashi for later use, season with a small amount of tamari soy sauce or a pinch of sea salt to prevent spoilage. Refrigerate to store.

Prepared Dressings and Mayonnaise

In most natural food stores you can find a variety of prepared salad dressings and mayonnaises. Many of these products contain a large amount of oil, spices, herbs, and other ingredients not recommended for regular use. As with other foods, fresh homemade dressings are always the best for regular use. For those in good health, some of these products can be enjoyed on special occasions. However, as with all prepared foods, please read the label to see what ingredients are included when deciding whether a particular product is appropriate or not. Commercial salad dressings, including those served at most salad bars, may contain sugar, poor quality oil, dairy products, artificial vinegar, eggs, and chemical additives. They are best avoided by the health-conscious consumer.

When to Add Dressings

Salad dressings are usually prepared in advance but not added to the salad until just before serving. If left on the salad for too long, the dressing may cause lettuce and other greens to wilt. If the salad ingredients are to be marinated, then it is fine to add the dressing in advance so that the vegetables can absorb the marinade.

Miso Dressings
Miso-based dressings add a combination of salty, sweet, and slightly sour or fermented flavors to your salads. Miso can be combined with various other ingredients to prepare a variety of delicious dressings and dips. Miso dressings go very well with raw salads, tofu salads, crudités, boiled mixed salads, or simple salads. They are especially nice with wakame sea vegetable salads.

Miso dressings are simple and quick to prepare, often taking only 2 to 3 minutes. Generally, when adding miso dressings to salads, a tablespoon or so is enough for each serving.

Miso-Brown Rice Vinegar Dressing

$1\frac{1}{2}$ **Tbsp. barley miso**
1 Tbsp. brown rice or sweet brown rice vinegar
2 Tbsp. minced chives, parsley, or scallions
$\frac{1}{2}$ **tsp. grated onion**
2 tsp. mirin
$\frac{1}{2}$ **cup water**

Place the chives, parsley, or scallions in a suribachi and grind several seconds. Add the miso and purée to a smooth paste. Add the grated onion, vinegar, and mirin. Purée again until smooth. Then add water and purée until smooth.

Miso-Mustard Dressing

> 1½ Tbsp. barley miso
> 1 tsp. prepared miso mustard or natural yellow mustard
> 1 tsp. grated onion
> 1 Tbsp. minced parsley
> ½ cup water

Prepare as above.

Miso-Ginger Dressing

> 1½ Tbsp. barley miso
> 1 tsp. ginger juice
> 1 Tbsp. minced parsley
> ½ cup water

Prepare as above.

Miso-Tahini Dressing

> 1 tsp. barley miso
> 3 tsp. tahini (organic, roasted)
> 1 tsp. grated onion
> 1 tsp. minced parsley
> ½ cup water

Prepare as above.

Miso-Lemon Dressing

> 1 Tbsp. barley miso
> 1½ tsp. lemon juice
> 1 Tbsp. minced parsley
> ½ cup water

Prepare as above.

Miso-Orange Dressing

> 1 Tbsp. barley miso
> ¼ cup fresh orange juice
> 1 tsp. minced parsley or watercress

½ cup water

Prepare as above.

Miso-Umeboshi Vinegar Dressing

1 Tbsp. barley miso
1 tsp. umeboshi vinegar
1 Tbsp. chopped scallions or chives
½ cup water

Prepare as above.

Miso-Ume-Tahini Dressing

1 Tbsp. barley miso
1 tsp. umeboshi vinegar
3 tsp. organic, roasted tahini
2 tsp. chopped scallions, chives, or onion
½ cup water

Prepare as above.

Miso-Apple Dressing

2 Tbsp. grated apple
1½ Tbsp. barley miso
1 tsp. organic, roasted tahini
½ cup water

Prepare as above.

White Miso-Sesame Seed Dressing

1½ Tbsp. white miso
¼ cup roasted sesame seeds (tan)
1 tsp. chopped parsley
½ cup kombu dashi or water

Place the sesame seeds in a suribachi and grind to a smooth paste. Add the chopped parsley and grind again. Add the miso and purée until smooth. Next, add the dashi or water and purée until smooth.

Miso-Walnut Dressing

¼ cup roasted, finely chopped walnuts
1 Tbsp. barley miso

    1 tsp. minced parsley
    ½ cup water

Prepare as above.

Miso-Mirin-Vinegar Dressing

    1½ Tbsp. white, yellow, or barley miso
    2 tsp. mirin
    1 tsp. brown rice vinegar
    1 tsp. minced parsley
    1 Tbsp. saké
    ½ cup water

Place the parsley in a suribachi, and grind several seconds. Add the miso and purée until smooth. Next, place the saké, mirin, and vinegar in the suribachi and purée until smooth. Add water and purée again, until smooth.

Miso-Tofu-Tahini Dressing

    1½ Tbsp. barley miso
    ½ cup puréed tofu
    3 tsp. organic, roasted tahini
    1 Tbsp. chopped chives, scallions, or minced onion
    ⅓ cup water

Place the chives, scallion, or onion in a suribachi and grind several seconds. Add the miso and purée until smooth. Add the tahini, and grind again until mixed thoroughly. Add the tofu purée, and grind again until thoroughly mixed. Place the water in the suribachi, and purée until smooth and creamy. You may add more water for a thinner consistency if desired.

Tamari Soy Sauce Dressings and Marinades

Tamari soy sauce can be used as a base for preparing a wide variety of dressings or marinades. When you use tamari in dressings, the taste should be mild, such as it is in the dressings below. When you use it as a marinade for vegetables or fish, you may increase the amount of tamari and ginger indicated in the recipes, but only slightly.

Tamari soy sauce dressings can be used on just about any type of salad you prepare—grain, noodle, raw-vegetable, tofu, boiled-vegetable salads, or fish and seafood salads.

Hundreds of variations can be made with the basic proportions given below, simply by adding or combining other ingredients.

Most tamari soy sauce dressings are prepared in the same basic manner by simply mixing the various ingredients. If vegetables such as scallions, chives, parsley, or onion are added, first mince or chop them finely, then grind them in a suribachi before adding the remaining ingredients. If seeds or nuts are added, first roast, then chop them finely or coarsely, place them in a suribachi and grind until half-crushed before adding the remaining ingredients. When all of the ingredients have been added, simply mix well. Spoon over salads, rather than mixing in. Two or three teaspoons or so are usually sufficient for each serving. Below are a few tamari soy sauce dressing variations:

Tamari Soy Sauce-Scallion Dressing

> 1 Tbsp. tamari soy sauce
> 1 Tbsp. chopped scallions, chives, onions, or parsley
> $\frac{1}{2}$–$\frac{2}{3}$ cup water or dashi

Tamari Soy Sauce-Mustard Dressing

> 1 Tbsp. tamari soy sauce
> 1 tsp. prepared mustard
> 1 Tbsp. chopped or minced parsley
> $\frac{1}{2}$–$\frac{2}{3}$ cup water

Tamari Soy Sauce-Ginger Dressing

> 1 Tbsp. tamari soy sauce
> $\frac{1}{4}$–$\frac{1}{3}$ tsp. ginger or ginger juice
> $\frac{1}{2}$–$\frac{2}{3}$ cup water

Tamari Soy Sauce-Lemon Dressing

> 1 Tbsp. tamari soy sauce
> 1 tsp. fresh lemon or lime juice
> 1 Tbsp. chopped or minced parsley
> $\frac{1}{2}$–$\frac{2}{3}$ cup water

Tamari Soy Sauce-Orange Dressing

> 1 Tbsp. tamari soy sauce
> $\frac{1}{4}$ cup fresh orange juice
> 1 Tbsp. chopped or minced parsley
> $\frac{1}{2}$–$\frac{2}{3}$ cup water

Tamari Soy Sauce-Umeboshi Vinegar Dressing

> 1 Tbsp. tamari soy sauce
> $1\frac{1}{2}$ tsp. umeboshi vinegar
> 2 tsp. mirin
> $\frac{1}{2}$–$\frac{2}{3}$ cup water

1 tsp. chopped parsley, scallion, or chives

Tamari Soy Sauce-Vinegar Dressing

1 Tbsp. tamari soy sauce
1–1½ tsp. brown rice or sweet rice vinegar
1 Tbsp. chopped or minced parsley, chives, or scallions
½–⅔ cup water

Tamari Soy Sauce-Mirin Dressing

1 Tbsp. tamari soy sauce
1–1½ tsp. brown rice vinegar
1 Tbsp. chopped or minced parsley
2 tsp. mirin
½–⅔ cup water

Tamari Soy Sauce-Sesame Dressing

1 Tbsp. tamari soy sauce
1–1½ tsp. brown rice or sweet rice vinegar
2 Tbsp. roasted, ground, tan sesame seeds
1 Tbsp. chopped or minced parsley
½–⅔ cup water

As a variation, roasted, chopped and ground walnuts, pecans, sunflower or pumpkin seeds can be substituted for sesame seeds.

Tamari Soy Sauce-Dashi Dressing

1 Tbsp. tamari soy sauce
2 tsp. mirin
¼–⅓ tsp. grated ginger or ginger juice
1 Tbsp. chopped or minced parsley, scallion or chives
½–⅔ cup kombu dashi

Tamari Soy Sauce-Bonito Flake Dressing

1 Tbsp. tamari soy sauce
¼ tsp. grated ginger or ginger juice
1 Tbsp. chopped or minced parsley, scallions, or chives
½–⅔ cup kombu-bonito flake dashi

Tamari Soy Sauce, Oil, and Vinegar Dressing

1 Tbsp. tamari soy sauce
3–4 Tbsp. brown rice or sweet rice vinegar
1 Tbsp. grated onion

¼–½ tsp. light sesame oil (heated)
1–2 Tbsp. roasted tan sesame seeds, chopped
1 tsp. chopped or minced parsley
½ cup water

Umeboshi Dressings

Umeboshi-based dressings add a nice sour-salty taste to your salads. They have a very light, refreshing taste that is especially nice in the spring and summer. Umeboshi-based dressings are alkaline, whereas other vinegar-based dressings are more acid, thus making umeboshi dressings suitable for those in good health as well as those with health problems.

Umeboshi dressings are appropriate for any kind of salad. They can be mixed into salads just before serving or spooned over them when served.

Umeboshi-Parsley Dressing

2 umeboshi plums, pits removed
1 tsp. minced parsley
½ tsp. grated onion
¼ tsp. light sesame oil, heated (optional)
¾ cup water or kombu dashi

Place the umeboshi plums in a suribachi and grind to a smooth paste. Add the parsley and onion. Grind again. Add the oil and purée. Add the water to the other ingredients, and purée again.

Umeboshi-Scallion Dressing

¼ cup chopped scallions or chives
2 umeboshi plums, pits removed
¾ cup water or kombu dashi

Prepare as above.

Umeboshi-Sesame Seed Dressing

2 umeboshi plums, pits removed
2 Tbsp. roasted sesame (tan or black), sunflower, or pumpkin seeds
1 tsp. parsley, minced
¾ cup water or kombu dashi

Place the sesame seeds in a suribachi, and grind until half-crushed. If using sunflower or pumpkin seeds, chop first, then grind as above. Add the umeboshi plums, and grind to a smooth paste. Place the parsley and water in the suribachi, and purée.

Umeboshi-Daikon Dressing

> 2 umeboshi plums, pits removed
> 1 Tbsp. grated daikon
> 1 tsp. chopped parsley or scallions
> ¾ cup water or kombu dashi

Place the umeboshi in a suribachi, and purée to a smooth paste. Add the daikon and parsley or scallions. Grind again. Add the water or kombu dashi and mix thoroughly.

Umeboshi-Lemon or Orange Dressing

> 2 umeboshi plums, pits removed
> 1 tsp. fresh lemon juice or 2–3 Tbsp. fresh orange juice
> 1 Tbsp. minced parsley
> ¾ cup water or kombu dashi

Combine all ingredients and mix well.

Umeboshi Vinegar-Miso Dressing

> 1 tsp. umeboshi vinegar
> 1 Tbsp. barley miso
> 3 tsp. organic, roasted tahini
> 2 tsp. chopped scallions or chives
> ½–¾ cup water or kombu dashi

Place the miso and tahini in a suribachi and grind to a smooth paste. Add the umeboshi vinegar and scallions or chives. Grind again. Add water and purée until smooth.

Umeboshi-Brown Rice Vinegar Dressing

> 2 Tbsp. umeboshi vinegar
> 1 tsp. brown rice or sweet rice vinegar
> 1 tsp. mirin
> 1 Tbsp. chopped parsley, scallions, or chives
> ¾ cup water or kombu dashi

Mix ingredients thoroughly and serve.

Umeboshi-Tahini Dressing

> 2–3 umeboshi plums, pits removed
> 2–3 Tbsp. organic, roasted tahini
> 1 tsp. grated onion
> 1 Tbsp. chopped scallion, chives, or parsley

¾ **cup water**

Pureé the umeboshi plums in a suribachi until smooth. Add the tahini and purée again. Add remaining ingredients and purée until smooth and creamy.

Umeboshi-Bonito Flake Dressing

> **2 umeboshi plums, pits removed or 2 Tbsp. umeboshi vinegar**
> ¾ **cup kombu-bonito flake dashi**
> **1 Tbsp. chopped parsley, scallions, or chives**

Place the plums and parsley, scallions or chives in a suribachi, and purée until a smooth paste. Add the kombu-bonito flake dashi and mix thoroughly.

Sea Salt Dressings

Because of its harsh quality, raw or uncooked salt is rarely used in homemade salad dressings. Occasionally, however, sea salt can be used as a base for dressings if it is first diluted in water and boiled for several minutes. Below is a recipe showing how to do this:

Sea Salt-Brown Rice Vinegar Dressing

> ½ **tsp. sea salt**
> **2 tsp. brown rice or sweet brown rice vinegar**
> **1 tsp. roasted sesame seeds, tan or black**
> **1 Tbsp. minced parsley, scallions, or chives**
> ¾ **cup water or kombu dashi**

Place the sea salt and water in a saucepan and bring to a boil. Reduce the flame to low, cover, and simmer for 7 to 10 minutes. Remove and allow to cool. Grind the sesame seeds in a suribachi until half-crushed. Add the parsley, scallions or chives, and grind again. Mix in the vinegar and salted water or dashi. Mix well.

Tofu Dressings

Firm- or hard-style tofu can be used as a base for making smooth, creamy dressings that are usually big favorites. Tofu dressings can be used on noodle, raw- or cooked-vegetable, sea-vegetable, or seafood salads. They can be mixed in just before serving or spooned over when served. When preparing tofu dressings for regular use, we recommend puréeing them in a suribachi. For special occasions, when a large volume of dressing is needed, you may use a blender. This creates a very smooth texture, similar to that of tofu mayonnaise.

For those with health problems, it is better to boil the tofu for a minute or so and allow it to cool before using it.

Tofu-Umeboshi Dressing

> 1 cake (16 oz.) tofu
> 1 tsp. umeboshi paste or 3 umeboshi plums, pits removed
> 2 Tbsp. grated onion
> 1 Tbsp. chopped scallions, chives, or parsley
> ¼–½ cup water

Place the umeboshi paste or plums in a suribachi and grind to a smooth consistency. Add the onion and scallions, chives, or parsley. Mix in. Place the tofu in a hand food mill and purée. Add the puréed tofu to the suribachi and mix in thoroughly with the umeboshi and scallions. Add water and purée until smooth and creamy.

Tofu-Miso Dressing

> 1½ Tbsp. barley miso
> 3 tsp. organic, roasted tahini
> ½ cake (8 oz.) fresh, hard-style tofu
> 1 Tbsp. minced chives or scallions
> ⅓–¾ cup water

Place all ingredients in a blender, and purée to a smooth, creamy consistency.

Tofu-Cheese Dressing
Place the tofu cheese (refer to the previous chapter for instructions on making) in a blender. Add 1/2 to 3/4 cup of water, 1 tablespoon chopped chives, scallions or parsley, and purée until smooth and creamy.

Tofu Mayonnaise
Store-bought, prepared tofu mayonnaise can be enjoyed once in a while by those in good health, but is not recommended for regular use. To prepare your own tofu mayonnaise, simply place one of the above dressings in a blender and purée until creamy.

Variations: For variety in the above recipes, try adding roasted, ground sesame seeds, or substitute tamari soy sauce for umeboshi or miso. Tofu cheese can be made by marinating tofu in a mixture of water and tamari soy sauce or water and umeboshi vinegar instead of packing it in miso. Please experiment.

Other Dressings

Green Goddess Dressing
This smooth, creamy dressing uses cooked brown rice as a base.

> 2–3 umeboshi plums, pits removed

    1 cup water
    2 Tbsp. minced or grated onion
    ¾ cup cooked brown rice
    ½ cup finely chopped parsley
    2 Tbsp. organic roasted tahini
    1 Tbsp. tamari soy sauce

Boil the umeboshi plums for 1 minute in 1 cup of water. Add the onion and boil for 1 minute. Place the rice, parsley, water, umeboshi, and onion in a blender. Add the tahini and tamari soy sauce. Purée to a smooth, creamy consistency.

    As a variation, try adding a little sweet brown rice vinegar for a different flavor.

Daikon-Cucumber-Lemon Dressing

    ½ cup grated daikon
    ½ cup grated cucumber, ends removed
    1–2 tsp. fresh lemon juice
    ½ tsp. tamari soy sauce

Combine the ingredients. For a thinner dressing add water to desired consistency.

Dips

For crudités (finger food) salads, you may want to serve dips instead of dressings. The following are just a few suggestions and recipes.

Tofu Dips

Any of the above tofu dressings can serve as dips. Simply omit water from the recipe for a thicker consistency.

Hummus

    2 cups cooked chick-peas
    1 medium onion, diced or grated
    2 Tbsp. chopped or minced parsley
    2 umeboshi plums, pits removed
    2–3 Tbsp. organic, roasted tahini (optional)
    Chopped scallions or chives for garnish

Purée onion, parsley, and umeboshi in a suribachi. Add the tahini, and purée again. Purée the chick-peas, using most of the chick-pea cooking water, in a hand food mill. Mix the puréed chick-peas with the other ingredients in the suribachi. Purée until creamy and smooth. Place in a bowl, or fill carved out lemon or cucumber boats with the hummus. Garnish with chopped scallions or chives.

Lentil Pâté
Lentil pâté can be prepared in the same manner as hummus. First cook the lentils. Substitute a small amount of barley miso for the umeboshi in the above recipe. Use all other ingredients (except chick-peas) from the above recipe. Purée until smooth and creamy.

Chapter 6

Whole Grain and Pasta Salads

A wide variety of whole grains and grain products can be used to prepare delicious and attractive salads. Some of the whole grains used most frequently in salads include brown rice, wild rice, barley, millet, wheat products such as couscous and bulgur, corn on the cob, and buckwheat, or kasha. Whole grain noodles, such as *udon*, *somen*, soba, and whole wheat spaghetti and pastas can also be used in making light and delicious salads.

Whole grains are first cooked and then combined with other ingredients to make salads. They can be seasoned with condiments or dressings just before serving. Whole grain and noodle salads are especially refreshing in warmer weather. They can be served at room temperature or slightly chilled.

Brown Rice

Brown rice may be divided into three main types: short, medium, and long grain. Short-grain rice is the most suitable of the three for daily use in a temperate, or four-season climate. It is chewier, more glutenous, and a little stickier than the other varieties. It is the staple grain in most macrobiotic households. Medium-grain rice is slightly longer and thinner than short grain, and when cooked, is lighter and a little more fluffy. It can be eaten in warmer weather by itself or combined with short-grain rice. Long-grain rice is the lightest and fluffiest of the three. It is used more in warmer regions or during the summer, and can be combined with short-grain rice to create variety in your salads.

Brown rice can be cooked in a variety of ways to produce different tastes and textures. The basic methods of rice cooking that are used when making salads are discussed below.

Pressure-cooking—This is the most frequently used method of preparing brown rice. Pressure-cooked rice retains more nutrients and is sweeter and easier to digest than rice cooked with other methods.

There are many ways to pressure-cook brown rice. The method we recommend for the sweetest and richest-tasting rice is as follows: Wash the rice as instructed in Chapter 3. Place in a pressure cooker with 1 1/4 to 1 1/2 cups of water per cup of grain. Next, place the uncovered pressure cooker on a low flame for 10 to 15 minutes or until the water comes to a boil. Then add a small pinch of sea salt for each cup of rice, and place the lid on the cooker. Turn the flame to high, and bring up to pressure. When the pressure is up, the pressure gauge will begin to jiggle and make a hissing sound. At this time reduce the flame to medium-low and place a metal flame deflector under the cooker. Pressure-cook for 50 minutes.

When the rice is done, remove from the burner and gently place a chopstick under the pressure gauge on top of the lid. This will allow the pressure to escape a little faster than usual, and gives the rice a slightly lighter quality. When the pressure is fully released, remove the lid, and let the rice sit for 4 to 5 minutes to loosen the rice at the bottom of the cooker. Take a wooden rice paddle and moisten it slightly with cold water. Remove the rice one paddleful at a time and place it in a wooden bowl, smoothing each paddleful with several strokes of the paddle as it is placed in the bowl. Continue until all the rice is in the bowl.

To cool the rice more quickly, and to make it more fluffy for salads, keep mixing it by making strokes through it with the paddle, allowing heat to escape. When the rice is cool, it is ready to use in salads.

Boiling—This method of cooking brown rice is especially popular in warmer weather, as it produces rice with a light, fluffy texture. Boiled rice is less sweet than pressure-cooked rice, and some nutrients may escape in the steam.

To prepare boiled rice, first wash the grain. Then place it in a heavy pot and add 2 cups of water per cup of rice. Add a pinch of sea salt for each cup of grain, and cover with a heavy lid to keep moisture in. Turn the flame to high, and bring to a boil. Reduce the flame to medium-low, and simmer for 60 minutes or until all water has been absorbed by the rice. It is best not to uncover the rice as it is cooking, in order to prevent moisture from escaping and making the rice too dry.

Use the instructions given above for removing the rice from the pot.

Pre-roasting—On occasion, brown rice can be dry-roasted before it is cooked to produce a slightly drier and chewier dish. To roast brown rice, wash it, and then dry-roast in a stainless-steel skillet, stirring constantly, as if you were roasting sesame seeds. Roast until the rice turns golden colored and releases a slightly nutty aroma. Remove immediately from the hot skillet to prevent scorching, and then either pressure-cook or boil.

To pressure cook, place the rice in the cooker with 1 1/2 cups of water per cup of roasted grain. Add a pinch of sea salt per cup of rice. Cover and bring up to pressure over a high flame. When the pressure is up, reduce the flame to medium-low, place a flame deflector under the cooker, and cook for 30 to 40 minutes.

To boil the roasted rice, place it in a pot, add 2 cups of water per cup of rice, and cover. Add a pinch of sea salt per cup of grain, cover, and bring to a boil. Reduce the flame to medium-low and simmer for about 30 to 40 minutes. Remove the rice as instructed above.

Once the rice cools, it is now ready to be combined with a variety of other ingredients in salads.

Brown Rice Salad #1

> **4 cups cooked brown rice**
> **$\frac{1}{2}$ cup sweet corn, removed from the cob**
> **$\frac{1}{2}$ cup sweet green peas**
> **$\frac{1}{4}$ cup carrots, sliced in thin matchsticks**
> **$\frac{1}{4}$ cup celery, diced**
> **Pinch of sea salt**
> **Brown rice vinegar**

Place about 1 inch of water in a pot and bring to a boil. Add the sweet corn, and boil for 2 to 3 minutes or until tender and sweet. Remove, drain, and allow to cool. Next, place the fresh green peas in the same boiling water that the corn was cooked in. Cover, and boil several minutes, until tender and bright green in color. Remove, drain, and allow to cool. Place the carrots in the boiling water, cover, and simmer 1 to 2 minutes. Remove, drain, and allow to cool. Then place the celery in the same boiling water, cover, and simmer 1 to 2 minutes. Remove, drain, and allow to cool.

Mix all the vegetables together in a bowl. Add a pinch of sea salt, and sprinkle brown rice vinegar over them. Mix well, and allow to marinate for about 30 minutes. Mix the vegetables together with the cooked brown rice so that they are evenly distributed throughout the rice. Place the salad in a serving bowl and garnish. The salad may be served room temperature or slightly cool.

Brown Rice Salad #2

> **4 cups cooked brown rice**
> **$\frac{1}{2}$ cup carrots, sliced in thin matchsticks**
> **$\frac{1}{4}$ cup yellow wax beans, sliced on a very thin diagonal**
> **$\frac{1}{2}$ cup green string beans, sliced on a very thin diagonal**
> **$\frac{1}{4}$ cup burdock, shaved or sliced in thin matchsticks**

½ cup deep-fried tofu, drained, and sliced in thin strips
Tamari soy sauce
2 shiitake mushrooms, soaked 10 minutes, stemmed, and sliced very thin, or diced
2 tsp. barley malt
Pinch of sea salt
½ fresh lemon
Several fresh, raw lettuce leaves, washed and drained

Place about 1 inch of water in a pot, and bring to a boil. Boil the vegetables in the following order: carrots; yellow wax beans; green string beans; and burdock. Boil them in the same water, following the instructions for boiling, draining, and cooling presented in the recipe above. When cool, combine in a mixing bowl.

Place the deep-fried tofu in a small amount of boiling water, and season mildly with tamari soy sauce. Simmer for 5 to 6 minutes. Remove and place in the bowl with the vegetables.

Place the shiitake mushrooms in a saucepan with a small amount of boiling water, add the barley malt and several drops of tamari soy sauce for a mild salt flavor. Cover and simmer for 5 to 7 minutes. Remove and place in the bowl with the vegetables and tofu.

Sprinkle a pinch of sea salt over the cooked vegetables and tofu and squeeze several drops of fresh lemon juice over them. Mix well, and allow to marinate for 30 minutes or so.

Combine the vegetables, tofu, and shiitake mushrooms with the cooked brown rice, and mix thoroughly to distribute the ingredients evenly throughout the rice. Place the salad in a serving bowl lined with fresh, crisp lettuce leaves. Garnish and serve at room temperature or slightly cool.

Variations:

1.   Marinate vegetables in umeboshi vinegar instead or rice vinegar or lemon juice and sea salt.

2.   Instead of marinating the vegetables, simply combine the ingredients after cooking, and mix in a level teaspoon of finely chopped or minced shiso leaves.

3.   Use other combinations of vegetables.

4.   Use deep-fried tempeh, or strips of dried tofu which have been simmered several minutes in a little water and tamari soy sauce just as the fresh tofu is in the above recipe.

5.   Use tamari soy sauce-ginger dressing in place of brown rice vinegar or lemon juice.

Sushi

> **4 cups cooked brown rice**
> **4–5 sheets toasted nori**
> **1 cucumber, sliced in rounds, then sliced in matchsticks**
> **Several pieces of pickled red shiso leaves (packed in with umeboshi plums)**

Take 1 sheet of nori and place it on top of a bamboo sushi mat with the rough, dull side facing up. Wet your hands very slightly with cold water and spread 1 cup of cooked rice evenly on the sheet of nori. Leave 1/2 to 1 inch of the top and 1/4 to 1/2 of the bottom of the sheet of nori uncovered by rice. Take a bamboo rice paddle and wet it slightly. Press the rice down evenly with the dampened rice paddle.

Place a row of cucumber matchsticks 1 inch wide across the width of the rice, approximately 1 inch from the bottom of the sheet of nori. Then lay a thin row of shiso leaves across the width of the cucumbers, so that the leaves rest on top of them.

Use the sushi mat to roll up the rice and nori, pressing the mat firmly but gently against the rice and nori until it is completely rolled up into a round log shape. As you are rolling, your thumbs should be pressing against the bamboo mat, while the fingers, on both hands, should be tucking in the vegetables and pressing against the sheet of nori. As you are rolling forward, gradually pull the sushi mat backward so that it does not roll up inside the nori roll. Just before you reach the top

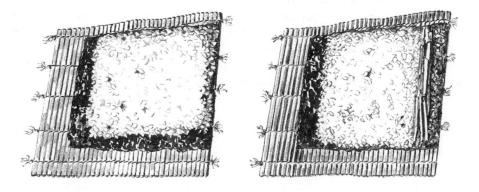

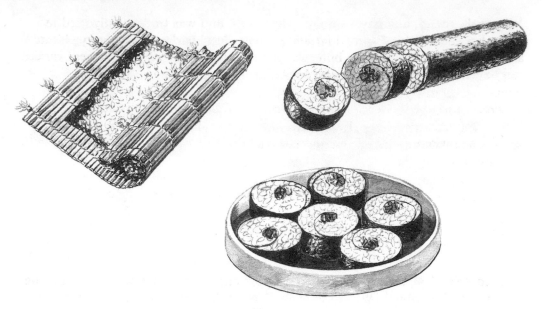

end of the sheet of nori, when rolling, wet your fingers slightly and moisten the end of the nori before you continue rolling. This will seal the nori securely around the rice and vegetables. Repeat this process again, until all ingredients are used up. You should now have four cylinder or log-shaped rolls.

Wet a very sharp knife and slice the rolls, one at a time, in half. Next, cut each half into four equal pieces of sushi. You should now have eight pieces of sushi per roll. If you do not wet your knife every time you slice the roll, the sushi will tear and fall apart and the rice will stick to the knife.

Arrange the sushi on a serving platter with the cut side facing up, showing the rice and vegetables. Garnish the platter, and serve with a dip sauce made of half water and half tamari soy sauce.

A wide variety of delicious sushi can be made at home with natural ingredients, including noodles and vegetables. Please refer to the other macrobiotic cookbooks for recipe ideas.

Barley

A traditional staple in Europe, the Middle East, and Egypt, this nourishing grain is available in the form of hulled barley, pearled barley, and pearl barley. In the hulled variety, the outside hull is removed but the inside grain—which contains vitamins and minerals—remains intact. Hulled barley is light tan in color. Pearled barley is more thoroughly refined, making it similar to white rice. Because of its refined quality, we do not use it as often as hulled barley. However, it can be used on occasion to make light and delicious barley salads. Pearl barley (*hato mugi*) is actually a different species of grain that originally grew wild but is now cultivated.

It is small, round, and has a smooth white shell, and was traditionally used to neutralize the effects of animal fat and protein. Pearl barley has a chewy texture and a stronger, slightly more bitter flavor than other barleys. Any of these varieties can be used in salads, and may be cooked as follows:

Pressure-cooked	*Water Content*	*Salt Content*	*Cooking Time*
Any Type Barley— 1 cup soaked 6–8 hours	1 1/4–1 1/2 cup	pinch	50 minutes

Boiled	*Water Content*	*Salt Content*	*Cooking Time*
Any Type Barley— 1 cup soaked 6–8 hours	2 cups	pinch	1 hour

To prepare barley, use the same basic instructions for pressure-cooking or boiling brown rice given above. When the barley has finished cooking, remove it in the same manner as rice and let it cool. It is now ready to use in salads.

Barley Salad

> **4 cups cooked barley**
> **½ cup onions, diced**
> **½ cup carrots, diced**
> **¼ cup celery, diced**
> **¼ cup shiitake mushrooms, soaked, diced, and cooked 10 minutes**
>   **in a little tamari soy sauce and water**
> **¼ cup chopped parsley**
> **½ cup cooked seitan, cubed**
> **Tamari soy sauce-ginger dressing**

Place 1/2 inch of water in a pot and bring to a boil. Add the onions and blanch for several seconds. Remove and drain. Add the carrots to the boiling water and blanch for 1 minute. Remove and drain. Place the celery in the same boiling water and blanch for several seconds. Remove and drain. Place the rice, onions, carrots, celery, shiitake, chopped parsley, and seitan in a mixing bowl. Mix thoroughly. Spoon a tamari soy sauce-ginger dressing over each serving.

Variations:
1. Use umeboshi-parsley dressing
2. Use deep-fried tempeh cubes in place of seitan

Millet ————————————————————————

Millet is a slightly sweet-tasting grain, with a somewhat drier and lighter texture than other grains. This small, round, yellow-colored grain has been a staple in many northern Asian, European, and some African countries. There are many varieties of millet, but only the yellow variety is available in the United States. Millet makes wonderfully delicious and light salads. It can be pressure-cooked or boiled, or can be dry-roasted until golden yellow prior to cooking for a lighter, nuttier flavored grain.

Pressure-cooked	*Water Content*	*Salt*	*Cooking Time*
1 cup plain or dry-roasted	1 1/4–1 1/2	pinch	12–15 minutes

Place the millet, water and sea salt in a pressure cooker, cover, and turn the flame to high. When the pressure is up, reduce the flame to medium-low, place a flame deflector under the cooker and pressure-cook for the length of time indicated above. When done, allow the pressure to come down and remove as you would brown rice.

Boiled	*Water Content*	*Salt*	*Cooking Time*
1 cup plain or dry-roasted	2 1/2–3 cups boiling water	pinch	30–35 minutes

Place the water and pinch of sea salt in a heavy pot and bring to a boil. Add the millet, cover, and reduce the flame to medium-low. Simmer for the length of time shown above. When done, remove as you would brown rice.

Millet and Chick-pea Salad

>4 cups cooked millet
>1 cup cooked chick-peas
>½ cup raw onion, minced
>½ cup green peas, boiled until tender
>¼ cup carrot, diced and blanched 1 minute
>1 Tbsp. burdock, finely chopped and boiled 2–3 minutes
>½ cup sweet corn, removed from cob and blanched 1–2 minutes
>Umeboshi-tahini dressing
>1 Tbsp. chopped parsley, scallions, or chives for garnish

Place the millet, chick-peas, onion, peas, carrot, burdock, and sweet corn in a bowl. Mix well. Just before serving, mix in umeboshi-tahini dressing and garnish with chopped parsley, scallions, or chives.

Wheat

Although a staple grain in many countries throughout the world, in its whole form, wheat is difficult to digest and requires thorough chewing. For this reason, it is consumed mainly in the form of flour, including products such as noodles, pastas, bread, and the like. Other partially milled wheat products, such as bulgur, couscous, and cracked wheat are common in Middle Eastern countries and can be used in making salads. They are especially delightful during the summer, as they have a light and fluffy quality.

Couscous—To prepare couscous, wash and place in a fine-mesh strainer or steamer. Add a pinch of sea salt. Place a small amount of water in a pot. Set the steamer down inside the pot. Cover the pot and bring to a boil. Reduce the flame to medium-low, and steam for about 10 minutes. When done, remove from the steamer and allow to cool by fluffing the couscous with a rice paddle or wooden spoon.

Bulgur—To prepare bulgur, wash first. Place 1 cup of bulgur in a pot, with a pinch of sea salt. Pour 2 to 2 1/2 cups of boiling water over the bulgur. Bring to a boil again, cover, reduce the flame to low, and simmer 15 to 20 minutes. Remove and cool by fluffing the grain as above.

Cracked Wheat—Prepare as you would bulgur.

Couscous Salad

> 4 cups cooked couscous
> 1 cup cooked chick-peas
> ¼ cup leeks, thinly sliced and blanched 1 minute
> ¼ cup red radish, sliced in thin rounds and blanched several seconds
> ¼ cup celery, diced and blanched 1 minute
> ½ cup green beans, sliced straight across about ¼ inch thick, blanched
>   1–2 minutes or until tender and bright green
> Several fresh lettuce leaves, washed
> Umeboshi-tahini dressing
> 1 Tbsp. chopped parsley

Place the couscous, chick-peas, leeks, red radish, celery, and green beans in a bowl. Mix well. Line a serving platter or bowl with the fresh lettuce leaves. Just before serving, mix in the umeboshi-tahini dressing and the salad attractively on the bed of lettuce leaves. Garnish with chopped parsley and serve.

Bulgur Salad

> 4 cups cooked bulgur
> ¼ cup chopped red cabbage, blanched 1–2 minutes
> ½ cup green string beans, sliced and blanched 2–3 minutes
> ½ cup carrots, diced and blanched 1–2 minutes
> ¼ cup yellow summer squash, sliced in half and then in thin half-moons,

and blanched 1–2 minutes
1 Tbsp. tamari-roasted sunflower seeds
Umeboshi-parsley dressing

Place all ingredients, except the dressing, in a mixing bowl and mix thoroughly. Just before serving, add the dressing, and mix again. Arrange in a serving bowl, garnish, and serve.

Buckwheat

Buckwheat, or kasha, is still eaten as a staple in Eastern Europe, Russia, and other parts of the world. It is a more contractive grain, and is used more in cold weather, but can be served in other seasons as well. To prepare buckwheat, first wash, then place 1 cup of buckwheat into 2 cups of water to which a pinch of sea salt has been added. Bring to a boil, cover, and reduce the flame to medium-low. Simmer for about 20 minutes, or until all water has been absorbed. When done, remove the buckwheat, place in a bowl, and fluff to cool with wooden spoons or chopsticks. When completely cool, it may be used in making salads.

Buckwheat Salad

4 cups cooked buckwheat
½ cup deep-fried tempeh cubes, simmered in water to cover and seasoned mildly
**   with tamari soy sauce during the last several minutes (approximate cooking**
**   time, 20 to 25 minutes)**
¼ cup red onion, sliced in very thin, half-moon rings
½ cup snow peas, sliced in half and blanched several seconds
½ cup kale, sliced and blanched 1–2 minutes
¼ cup sweet corn, blanched 1–2 minutes
¼ cup red radishes, quartered and blanched 1–2 minutes
¼ cup sauerkraut, chopped
¼ cup sauerkraut juice
Tamari-ginger-parsley dressing

Place all ingredients in a bowl, except the dressing. Mix thoroughly. Add the dressing just before serving, mixing it in well. Arrange in a serving bowl and garnish attractively.

Noodle and Pasta Salads

Although they are especially light and refreshing in the summer, noodle and pasta salads can be enjoyed any time of year. There are many types of whole grain

noodles and pastas to choose from, and they are all delicious in salads. We can divide noodles and pastas into two categories: Japanese noodles (whole wheat udon and somen, and buckwheat noodles, or soba); and various American or European whole wheat spaghetti and pastas. The Japanese noodles are usually made with salt, so sea salt does not need to be added when you cook them. American or European pastas usually do not contain salt, so you can add a pinch of sea salt to the water when you boil them.

All noodles and pastas are cooked in the same basic manner. Place the noodles, spaghetti, or pasta in a pot of boiling water. Stir occasionally to prevent lumping. Bring to a boil again, and reduce the flame to medium. Do not cover the pot. Simmer until the noodles or pasta are done. When done, break a piece in half. The inside of the noodle should be the same color as the outside. If the inside is still white and the outside is darker, cook them a little longer. When done, place in a strainer or colander, rinse until cool with cold water, and allow to drain for several minutes. They are now ready to use.

Udon or Somen Salad

> 1 package (8 oz.) udon or 2 packages somen, cooked, rinsed, and drained
> $\frac{1}{2}$ cup cucumber, quartered and sliced on a thin diagonal

> ¼ cup red radish, sliced in thin rounds
> ¼ cup celery, sliced on a thin diagonal
> 1 cup tofu, cubed and marinated 30 minutes in a solution of tamari soy sauce, water, and a dab of grated ginger
> ¼ cup red onion, halved and sliced in thin half-rings
> ¼ cup coarsely grated carrots (use Western-style box grater)
> Tamari-ginger-parsley dressing

Combine all ingredients, except the dressing, in a bowl, and mix well. The dressing may be mixed into the noodles just before serving or individually spooned over each serving.

Udon, Somen, or Soba Sushi

> 1 package (8 oz.) udon, somen, or jinenjo soba, cooked, rinsed and drained
> 3–4 sheets toasted nori
> 3–4 strips of scallion or several sprigs of cooked watercress
> Tamari-scallion dressing (for dip sauce)

Place a sheet of toasted nori on top of a bamboo sushi mat. Place the cooked noodles on top of the nori in a layer about 1 inch thick so that they cover about three-fourths of the sheet. Set strips of scallion or several sprigs of cooked watercress across the width of the nori about 2 inches from the bottom of the sheet.

Roll up and slice as you would rice sushi. Arrange attractively on a serving platter, with the sliced side of the sushi facing up.

Garnish the platter and serve with a tamari-scallion dressing (placed in small individual bowls or cups) for use by each person as a dip sauce.

Soba Salad

> 1 package (8 oz.) soba, cooked
> ½ cup deep-fried tofu cubes, drained and simmered in a little tamari soy sauce and water for 7–10 minutes
> ½ cup cucumber, sliced in rounds, then in thin matchsticks
> ½ cup carrots, sliced in matchsticks and blanched 1–2 minutes
> ¼ cup red radishes, sliced in thin rounds
> ¼ cup leeks, sliced thin and blanched 1–2 minutes
> ¼ cup toasted nori strips
> Tamari-scallion or chive dressing

Place the cooked soba, deep-fried tofu, and vegetables in a bowl. Mix well. Just before serving, garnish the salad with the toasted nori strips. While serving, spoon the dressing over each portion.

Whole Wheat Macaroni Salad

> 8 oz. whole wheat macaroni, cooked, rinsed, and drained

½ cup carrot, shredded
½ cup cucumber, sliced in thin quarters
¼ cup celery, sliced on a thin diagonal
¼ cup red onion, sliced in very thin, half-rings
¼ cup red radish, sliced in thin rounds
Chopped parsley garnish
Creamy tofu dressing

Place all ingredients, except the parsley and dressing, in a bowl and mix well. Just before serving, add the dressing and mix thoroughly. Garnish with chopped parsley.

Variations: Try any of the following dressings: tahini, umeboshi, tamari-ginger, or others. Use whole wheat spaghetti, shells, rigatoni, or other whole grain noodles, or use other combinations of cooked or raw vegetables.

Saifun or *Baifun* (Clear Mung Bean Thread Noodle) Salad
Saifun or baifun noodles, although not used often, are especially enjoyable as a special treat in summer. These clear noodles are made from mung beans, and are sometimes called "cellophane" noodles.

1 package saifun
Bonito flakes
Any tamari-based dressing

Place several cups of water in a pot and bring to a boil. Turn off the flame and drop the saifun into the pot. Leave for several minutes. Remove, rinse under cold water, and allow to drain.

Place the noodles in a serving bowl and garnish with bonito flakes.

Serve with a tamari-based dressing, which each person can spoon over their salad.

Chapter 7

Fresh Vegetable Salads

The fresher your salad vegetables are, the better. The ideal situation would be to have your own vegetable garden, so that vegetables are picked fresh daily. If this is not practical, at least try to find a good source of fresh produce. If your salad vegetables are old, limp, or wilted, your salads may not be as well received as they could be.

Whenever possible, purchase vegetables that are grown organically, without artificial fertilizers or pesticides. Organic produce has the best flavor and is better for your health. It is also important to wash your vegetables thoroughly. Improperly cleaned vegetables detract from the beauty and flavor of your salads. Needless to say, irradiated vegetables are not recommended for use in healthful salads or in other dishes.

Varieties

Vegetables come in three basic types: leafy green, ground, and root varieties, as explained below.

1. **Leafy greens** range in color from light to dark green, while a few varieties have a slightly reddish tinge on their leaves. Greens add freshness and strong upward energy to meals. Light-colored greens are generally milder and less fibrous than more deep-green varieties, which often have more bitter or pungent flavors. Lighter-colored greens are usually softer and more watery than darker-colored ones, and cook more quickly. A wide variety of leaf structures also exists. Some greens have smooth, large leaves, some are more crinkled or curled, while others are minutely detailed (such as parsley and carrot tops). Younger leaves are often less fibrous and bitter tasting than older ones. Most greens are bitter or pungent in their raw state but become milder or sweeter when cooked.

When cooking greens, it is important to use seasonings properly. For instance, when cooked with a pinch of salt, strong-tasting greens such as watercress, mustard greens, turnip greens, daikon greens, dandelion greens, radish greens, endive, escarole, chicory, parsley, and carrot tops, become very bitter or pungent. It is better to cook these greens without adding salt to the cooking water. On the other hand, milder greens such as kale, Chinese cabbage, green cabbage, and collards become sweeter when a pinch of salt is added just before they are finished cooking.

Below we present some of the greens used in macrobiotic salad preparation, together with their primary flavors:

> Watercress—pungent, slightly bitter
> Cress (most types)—pungent
> Dandelion—bitter (older more bitter)
> Alfalfa sprouts—mild
> Mustard greens—pungent, slightly bitter
> Turnip greens—mild
> Daikon greens—mild to pungent
> Oriental greens (of the mustard family):
>> Pak choi (celery mustard)—mildly pungent; smaller leaves are best in raw salads; larger leaves in boiled salads.
>> Bok choy—mild
>> *Mizuna*—bitter
> Radish greens—mildly pungent
> Chinese cabbage—mildly sweet when cooked; pungent when raw
> Kale—coarse when raw; becomes tender and sweet when cooked; if steamed, it becomes more bitter.
> Green cabbage—sweet to occasionally pungent; dark outer leaves are more bitter.
> Chicory family:
>> Endive—bitter when raw; when blanched becomes milder.
>> Escarole—same as endive
>> Belgian endive—mild bitter, becomes sweeter when cooked.
>> Chicory—slightly bitter (sometimes called prickly lettuce)
> Lettuce (three types: tall, head, loose leafy or curled)—some are slightly bitter, but most are very mild.

Parsley—bitter; mild when cooked

Carrot tops—bitter; mild when cooked

Collards—best cooked, often softer and sweeter than kale

Wild plants—small, young ones are tender and mildly bitter, sour, or pungent. Older plants are tougher and more bitter. Please consult a good botanical textbook or with someone who is knowledgable about wild foods to determine which varieties are edible and how to use them.

Broccoli—although often classified as a ground vegetable, it can also be used as a green. It has a mildly sweet flavor.

Celery leaves—strong bitter or sour

Kohlrabi leaves—tough when raw, become tender and sweet when boiled.

2. **Ground vegetables** are those that grow above ground, many on bushes or vines. Ground vegetables are often sweeter than leafy greens and root vegetables. They add a nice, calm, centering and warming energy to the dishes we prepare. Ground vegetables usually take slightly longer to cook than leafy greens, but slightly less time than most root vegetables. Of course, the length of time needed for cooking depends on how the vegetable is sliced as well as its texture. Ground vegetables include cucumbers, scallions, chives, celery, peas, cauliflower, Brussels sprouts, broccoli, kohlrabi, corn, cabbages, string and wax beans, leeks, and a variety of squashes. Some of these may be used raw in salads, but most are better when cooked. Ground vegetables range from mildly bitter or pungent to sweet tasting. When cooked they become milder and sweeter. Compared to greens, ground vegetables come in a wider range of colors, flavors, and textures, making them indispensable in the art of salad preparation.

3. **Root vegetables** or those which grow below the ground, are also important in salad preparation. Their more contractive energies make wonderful balance with the expansive energy of leafy greens. Roots have stabilizing and strengthening qualities. Most are sweet, pungent, or bitter when raw, and become milder or sweeter when cooked. Their colors are usually white, orange, yellow or tan, brown, some red, and very occasionally black (black daikon). Some may be used raw in salads by grating or mincing them, but they can also be lightly cooked for a sweeter flavor in salads. Root vegetables include carrots, radishes, turnips, daikon, onions, rutabaga, parsnips, burdock, ginger, and lotus root. Special care needs to be taken when washing root vegetables, so as not to damage their delicate, nutrient-rich skins. Root vegetables are seldom peeled, except occasionally for special effects or if the skin is waxed.

For a more complete listing of vegetables used in macrobiotic salad preparation, please refer to Chapter 2.

Preparing Vegetables —————————————

Together with using raw vegetables in salads, a variety of lightly cooked or naturally processed vegetables can also be used. Vegetables can be quickly boiled or blanched, pressed, marinated, pickled, and occasionally steamed. Below are guidelines for using these cooking methods when preparing salads.

1.   Quick boiling or blanching—These methods of cooking are basically the same, with the major difference between them being that blanching usually takes only a few seconds, while quick boiling may take anywhere from 1 to 5 minutes, depending on the texture and thickness of the vegetable. Leafy greens are best quickly boiled on a high flame. High, medium, or low flame may be used for other types of vegetables. Greens may take from several seconds to a minute or so to cook, while ground or root vegetables usually take a little longer. Quick boiling and blanching remove strong bitter or pungent flavors, and make vegetables milder, sweeter, and easier to digest.

To quickly boil or blanch vegetables, first place water in a pot. For a larger quantity of vegetables, add about 2 to 3 inches of water. For smaller quantities, use about 1/2 to 1 inch. Bring to a boil. If you are cooking greens, place them in the pot, and when they are almost done, add a small pinch of sea salt to bring out their natural sweetness. (Salt can be omitted for the strong-tasting greens mentioned above.) If you are cooking ground or root vegetables, you may add a pinch of salt at the beginning. It is better to boil a small quantity of vegetables at a time to ensure even cooking. This may take a little longer, but it can make a big difference in the way your vegetables turn out.

When the vegetables have become tender, but still slightly crisp and brightly colored, remove and place them in a colander. Spread them out so that they cool more quickly. If you want them to cool more quickly so that they retain their bright colors, you may occasionally rinse them under cold water for a few seconds. Drain and use.

Sometimes, instead of cutting the greens before cooking, you can boil or blanch the whole leaves. Slice them after they have been cooked. This style of boiling is referred to in Japanese as *ohitashi*. Because the greens are not cut before being cooked, they retain more of their natural flavor and nutrients.

2.   Pressing, marinating, and pickling—These methods are also similar, with the main difference between them being the amount of time that is required. *Pressing* vegetables usually takes about 1 to 2 hours, depending on the choice of vegetables and how thinly you slice them. *Marinating* can take anywhere from several minutes to an hour. *Quick pickling* takes anywhere from 2 to 3 hours to 2 to 3 days, depending on how salty or sour you wish the pickles to become.

When making quick-pressed salads and pickles, it is important to slice the vegetables very thinly. If they are not thinly sliced, they require a longer time before being ready to eat. Freshness is also an important factor in successful pressing and pickling. Vegetables that are not fresh contain less water and may be tougher and wilted, making a less delicious dish and lengthening the amount of time needed for preparation.

To make pressed salads, first wash the vegetables well. Slice them very thinly, and place them in a pickle press (see the Glossary of Utensils at the end of the book) with any of the following natural pickling agents: sea salt; sea salt and brown rice vinegar; sea salt, mirin, and brown rice vinegar; umeboshi vinegar; tamari soy sauce, water, and brown rice vinegar; or other suitable combinations.

Mix the ingredients thoroughly, and place the cover on the press. Screw the top on tightly, and apply pressure by screwing the inside plate down. Let the vegetables sit until the water level rises above the pressure plate. When this happens, release some of the pressure, keeping the water level just under the pressure plate. If too much pressure is applied, the salad will not press properly, detracting from its flavor.

When done, remove the vegetables, squeeze out excess liquid, and if too salty, rinse quickly under cold water. Drain and arrange on a serving dish.

If you do not have a pickle press, take a large ceramic or glass bowl, and place the ingredients in it. Mix, and set a saucer or plate down inside the bowl so that it rests on the vegetables. Take a clean, heavy stone or a large jar filled with water, and set it on top of the plate for pressure. Let it sit for the same length of time indicated above (1 hour or so). If water rises above the plate, decrease the amount of weight until the water returns to just below the level of the plate. Follow the same basic steps for removing as above.

Marinating is simply a shorter version of pressing, in which vegetables are covered with marinade and allowed to sit for several minutes. Any of the salt or pickling agents presented above, or one of the tamari soy sauce, umeboshi, sea salt, or miso-based dressings in Chapter 5 can be used. If the vegetables are too salty after marinating, rinse them quickly under cold water.

To make quick pickles, wash vegetables and slice them thinly. Place them in a pickle press or bowl as indicated above. Add your pickling agent (any of those suggested above), and apply pressure. Let sit for 2 to 3 hours or even 2 to 3 days. The longer the pickles sit in a salty solution, the saltier and more sour they become. When done, remove, squeeze out any excess liquid, and if too salty, quickly rinse under cold water. They are now ready to serve.

The salty water that is left over can be saved and used in preparing dressings for boiled salads.

3. **Steaming**—Occasionally, steamed vegetables can be used in salads. Steaming greens may require experimenting, though, because some greens become more bitter when steamed. To steam vegetables, place about 1/2 inch of water in a pot. Set a collapsible, stainless-steel steamer basket down inside the pot, or place a bamboo steamer basket on top of the pot. Place the vegetables in the basket, cover, and bring the water to a boil. Steam several seconds to several minutes, depending on the vegetable, until tender but slightly crisp and brightly colored. Remove, allow to cool, or rinse under cold water, and allow to drain. The vegetables are now ready to use.

Boiled Salads

When preparing quickly boiled or blanched salads, you can use the same water to boil all of the vegetables in, but it is important to follow a certain order. For instance, in mixed salads, where several types of vegetables are used, boil those with the mildest flavors first, and those with the strongest flavors last, so as not to influence the flavor of the cooking water. Onions, Chinese cabbage, carrots, daikon root, summer squash, and kale leave mild flavors in the cooking water, and can be boiled first. Cabbage, radishes, squash, rutabaga and collards have a slightly stronger flavor, but are still fairly mild. They can be boiled after the very mild vegetables. Celery, parsley, parsnips, Brussels sprouts, mustard and daikon greens, burdock, carrot tops, and watercress leave stronger flavors in the water, and if boiled too soon, may cause the other vegetables in your salad to take on a bitter flavor.

In the following recipes, the vegetables are listed from the mildest to the strongest. Simply boil or blanch in the order in which they appear in the recipe.

Simple Boiled Salad #1

$\frac{1}{2}$ cup carrots, sliced in matchsticks, boiled 1 minute
1 cup bok choy, sliced, boiled 1–2 minutes
1 bunch watercress, boiled whole for 45–50 seconds, removed, rinsed, drained, and sliced
Umeboshi-parsley-sesame dressing

Place vegetables in a bowl and mix. Arrange attractively on a serving platter. Spoon the dressing over each serving of salad, or mix in just before serving.

Simple Boiled Salad #2

1 cup red onion, sliced in wedges, boiled 1 minute
1 cup summer squash, sliced in $\frac{1}{4}$-inch-thick half-moons, boiled 1 minute or so
1 cup broccoli flowerettes, boiled 1–2 minutes
Tofu-umeboshi dressing

Place vegetables in a bowl after draining and mix. Mix in the dressing just before serving. Arrange the salad attractively in a serving bowl.

Burdock with Sesame Dressing

2 cups burdock, shaved and simmered until tender in a small amount of water and 2 tsp. brown rice vinegar
$\frac{1}{4}$ cup tan sesame seeds, dry-roasted
1 tsp. tamari soy sauce
Sprig of parsley

Place the sesame seeds in a suribachi and grind until half crushed. Add the tamari soy sauce and grind several seconds more. Place the shaved burdock in the suribachi, and mix well with the sesame seeds until coated. Remove and arrange attractively in a serving dish. Garnish with a sprig of parsley and serve.

Parsley with Pumpkin-seed Dressing

> 1 bunch of parsley, washed, boiled whole 1 minute, rinsed, drained,
>   and sliced in ½-inch lengths
> ¼ cup pumpkin seeds, dry-roasted and chopped coarsely
> 1 tsp. tamari soy sauce

Place the pumpkin seeds in a suribachi and grind until a coarse powder. Add the tamari soy sauce and mix in well. Place the chopped parsley in the suribachi, and mix thoroughly until evenly coated with the pumpkin-seed dressing. Remove and place in a serving dish. Garnish with a colorful garnish and serve.

Mixed Boiled Salad #1

> ¼ cup onion, sliced in wedges, boiled 1 minute
> ¼ cup yellow summer squash, sliced in ¼-inch-thick rounds,
>   boiled 1 minute or so
> ¼ cup carrots, sliced on a thin diagonal, boiled 1–1½ minutes
> 1 cup kale, chopped, boiled 1 minute, rinsed, and drained
> ¼ cup celery, sliced on a diagonal, boiled 1 minute
> ¼ cup sunflower seeds, dry-roasted and seasoned with tamari soy sauce
> Umeboshi-chive dressing

Place all ingredients in a bowl, except the dressing, and mix well. Just before serving, add the dressing, or each person may spoon it over their own salad.

Mixed Boiled Salad #2

> ¼ cup scallions, sliced in 2-inch lengths, boiled several seconds
> ¼ cup carrots, sliced in matchsticks, boiled 1 minute
> ¼ cup yellow wax beans, sliced in 1–2-inch lengths, and boiled
>   1–2 minutes or until tender
> 1 cup snow peas, stemmed, boiled several seconds
> ½ cup red radishes, quartered, boiled 1 minute
> Miso-orange dressing

Mix all vegetables together. Just before serving, mix in the dressing, or spoon it individually over each serving. Arrange in a serving dish.

Finger Food Salad (Crudités)

> 4–5 broccoli spears, boiled 1–2 minutes
> 4–5 carrot sticks, boiled 1 minute

4–5 cauliflower flowerettes, boiled 1½–2 minutes
4–5 green beans, stemmed, boiled 1–2 minutes
4–5 raw cucumber slices
Tofu, chick-pea, or lentil dip

Arrange each vegetable separately on a serving platter, with a small bowl of one of the above dips in the center of the platter. Each person may individually dip the finger foods in the dip.

Simple Pressed Salad #1

1 cup red radishes, sliced in thin rounds
½ tsp. sea salt
1 tsp. mirin
1 tsp. sweet brown rice vinegar
2 Tbsp. black sesame seeds, dry-roasted and chopped

Place the red radishes, sea salt, mirin, and vinegar in a pickle press. Mix and place the top on the press. Screw the pressure plate down to apply pressure. Let sit for 1 hour. Remove, squeeze to remove excess liquid, and place in a bowl. Add the chopped, roasted sesame seeds, and mix in well. Place the sesame-coated radishes in a serving dish.

Simple Pressed Salad #2

1 large cucumber, thinly sliced in rounds
2 tsp. umeboshi vinegar
¼ cup tan sesame seeds, dry-roasted
2 Tbsp. water

Place the cucumbers and umeboshi vinegar in a pickle press. Mix well. Place the top on the press and apply pressure. Let sit 45 minutes to 1 hour. Remove, and squeeze out excess liquid.

Place the sesame seeds in a suribachi and grind until the seeds become a thick paste. Add the water, and grind again until smooth and creamy. Place the cucumbers in the sesame mixture, and mix thoroughly to coat them. Arrange attractively in a serving dish.

Mixed Pressed Salad

¼ cup celery, sliced on a thin diagonal
½ cup cucumber, sliced in thin rounds
¼ cup red radishes, sliced in thin rounds
¼ cup red onion, sliced in thin half-moons or half-rings
1 cup Chinese cabbage, thinly shredded
¼–½ tsp. sea salt
1 tsp. brown rice vinegar

Place all ingredients in a pickle press, and mix thoroughly. Place the top on and apply pressure. Let sit about 1 hour or so. Remove, squeeze out excess liquid, and attractively arrange in a serving dish.

Marinated Lotus Root Salad

> **2 cups fresh lotus root, halved or quartered and sliced thin**
> **2 Tbsp. tamari soy sauce**
> **2 Tbsp. brown rice vinegar**
> **2 Tbsp. water**
> **2 Tbsp. mirin**
> **2 tsp. sesame seeds, dry-roasted**
> **1 Tbsp. scallions, very thinly sliced on a diagonal**
> **1–2 drops of fresh-squeezed ginger juice**

Mix all ingredients together in a bowl. Let sit for about 30 minutes. Remove, drain, and place in a serving dish.

Variation: Use 2 Tbsp. umeboshi vinegar, 1/4 tsp. ginger juice, 2 Tbsp. chopped parsley, and 2 Tbsp. water, instead of the tamari-sesame-scallion marinade.

Marinated Daikon and Carrot Salad

> **1 cup daikon, sliced in thin matchsticks**
> **$\frac{1}{2}$ cup carrots, sliced in thin matchsticks**
> **2 tsp. white miso**
> **1 tsp. mirin**
> **1 tsp. tamari soy sauce**
> **$\frac{1}{4}$ tsp. ginger juice**
> **1 Tbsp. water**
> **$\frac{1}{4}$ cup parsley, chopped**

Place the miso, mirin, tamari soy sauce, ginger juice, and water in a suribachi and purée. Add the daikon and carrots. Mix thoroughly. Allow to sit for 30 minutes. Remove and place in a serving dish. Garnish with chopped parsley.

Raw Vegetable Salads ─────────────

A raw salad made from a variety of crisp and fresh vegetables is a refreshing, light, and cooling dish to serve during warmer months of the year, or even to balance a hearty, warming meal in cooler months.

It is important to wash your salad vegetables thoroughly. The vegetables used in raw salads are usually sliced, but with soft, crispy lettuce, it is sometimes nice to tear the leaves, giving the salad a natural appearance.

Also, it is sometimes nice to combine raw vegetables with quickly pressed, marinated, or pickled vegetables for a variety of flavors and textures.

Fresh garden salads can be tossed, mixing the ingredients together, or each vegetable can be arranged so that it occupies its own section in the serving bowl or individual salad bowls. Since raw salads can be quickly prepared, and because they wilt easily, especially in warmer weather, it is best to prepare them just before serving for optimum flavor and texture.

Dressings can be mixed in just before serving or can be spooned individually over each serving. Any of the dressings in Chapter 5 can be substituted for the dressings suggested in the recipes. To prevent wilting, it is best to mix the dressing in just before serving, or spoon it over the salad while serving.

Tossed Salad

> **2 cups fresh lettuce, torn in bite-size pieces**
> $\frac{1}{2}$ **cup carrots, coarsely grated**
> $\frac{1}{2}$ **cup cucumbers, sliced in $\frac{1}{4}$-inch-thick rounds**
> $\frac{1}{4}$ **cup celery, sliced on a thin diagonal**
> $\frac{1}{4}$ **cup red radishes, quartered, or sliced in thin rounds**
> $\frac{1}{4}$ **cup pickled tofu, diced**
> **Green goddess dressing**
> $\frac{1}{4}$ **cup croutons**

Place vegetables and pickled tofu in a bowl and toss thoroughly. Place in a serving bowl. Spoon the dressing individually over each serving. Sprinkle a few croutons on top for garnish.

Fresh Garden Salad

> **2 cups Boston or Bibb lettuce, torn in bite-size pieces**
> **1 cup chicory or endive, torn in bite-size pieces**
> $\frac{1}{2}$ **cup watercress, sliced**
> $\frac{1}{4}$ **cup green string beans, sliced in 2-inch lengths, boiled 2–3 minutes**
> $\frac{1}{4}$ **cup tempeh, cut into 2-inch-long, thin strips, deep-fried until golden brown, then simmered 20 minutes in a small amount of water, tamari soy sauce, and a slice of fresh ginger**
> $\frac{1}{4}$ **cup cooked seitan, cubed**
> $\frac{1}{2}$ **cup cucumber, sliced in thick rounds**
> $\frac{1}{4}$ **cup red onion, halved, and sliced in thin half-rings**
> $\frac{1}{4}$ **cup yellow summer squash, halved, and sliced in $\frac{1}{4}$-inch-thick half-moons, boiled 1 minute or so**
> **Creamy miso-tofu dressing**

Arrange each item in its own section in a salad bowl or on a platter. Spoon dressing individually over each serving.

Waldorf Salad

    3½ cups very finely shredded cabbage
    ¼ cup coarsely grated carrots
    ½ cup walnuts, roasted and chopped
    ¼ cup celery, sliced on a thin diagonal
    1 cup apple, cut in ¼-inch-thick chunks
    ¼ cup raisins
    ¼ cup seedless red grapes
    Tofu-sesame dressing

Place all ingredients in a bowl, except the dressing, and mix well. Just before serving, mix in the dressing. Place in a serving bowl.

Mung Bean Sprout Salad

    3 cups romaine, Boston, or Bibb lettuce, torn in bite-size pieces
    1 cup mung bean sprouts, boiled several seconds, rinsed, and drained
    ¼ cup water chestnuts, peeled, sliced in thin rounds, and boiled several seconds,
        rinsed, and drained
    ¼ cup fresh shiitake mushrooms, quartered, simmered 5–7 minutes in a small
        amount of water lightly seasoned with tamari soy sauce, drained
    ¼ cup slivered almonds, toasted
    Tamari-ginger-scallion dressing

Place all vegetables and the almonds in a bowl, and toss well. Just before serving, mix in the dressing.

Simple Cucumber salad

    2–3 fresh, unwaxed cucumbers
    Sea salt-vinegar-sesame oil dressing

Take a fork and draw it down the length of the cucumber skin, until the entire cucumber has been scored with shallow lines. Remove the ends of the cucumbers. Slice the cucumbers in thin rounds. Combine with dressing just before serving.

Watercress Salad with Creamy Tofu Dressing

    2 bunches watercress, washed and sliced
    Creamy tofu-umeboshi dressing

Just before serving, combine the watercress and tofu dressing. Place in a serving bowl.

Vegetable Aspics

Although they can be served any time of year, there is nothing like a refreshingly cool aspic on a hot summer day. Aspics are cooked vegetable, bean, noodle-and-vegetable, or grain-and-vegetable combinations cooked with a clear, tasteless sea vegetable called agar-agar. Agar-agar acts as a jelling agent and produces the same effect as commercial gelatin. However, unlike commercial gelatin, it contains no sugar and is a vegetable-quality product. Agar-agar comes in the form of flakes, powder, and bars, and is available at most natural and macrobiotic food stores. Please read the directions on the package carefully, because cooking instructions vary with each type of agar-agar and each brand. Agar-agar is also used in preparing fruit kantens and as a base for jams and marmalades.

In the following recipes we suggest using agar-agar flakes, as they are easier to use and are widely available. You may substitute the other forms of agar-agar in place of the flakes if you wish.

Vegetable aspics can be prepared in several ways:

1. Slice vegetables, then cook, and pour into a dish or mold.
2. Cook vegetables, then purée, and pour into a dish or mold.
3. Layer the vegetables between layers of clear, seasoned agar-agar.
4. Vegetable or sea-vegetable broths can be used as a liquid base for the aspic, or plain, clear aspics can be made.
5. Aspics can be served in individual cups or dishes, sliced in squares just before serving, or spooned into individual dishes.
6. Any vegetable aspic may be served plain or with a miso, tamari soy sauce, or umeboshi-based dressing spooned over each serving.

In this chapter we include only vegetable aspics. Recipes for bean aspics and kanten are presented in the chapters that follow.

Clear Aspic

> 4–5 cups water, or kombu dashi
> Pinch of sea salt
> 5–6 Tbsp. agar-agar flakes

Place the water in a saucepan with the sea salt and agar-agar flakes. Stir frequently to dissolve the flakes. Bring to a boil. Reduce the flame to low, and simmer 2 to 3 minutes. Pour the hot liquid into a shallow, glass baking dish. Place in a cool place or refrigerate until jelled. When the aspic has completely jelled, cut into small 1-inch squares, which can be added to vegetable or fruit salads, or slice into 3-inch squares, and serve with a tamari-ginger-scallion dressing.

Sliced Vegetable Aspic

   ½ cup onions, diced
   ½ cup carrots, sliced in matchsticks or flowers
   ¼ cup sweet corn, removed from cob
   ¼ cup green peas, removed from shell
   ½ cup celery, sliced on a thin diagonal
   4 cups kombu dashi, or vegetable stock
   5–6 Tbsp. agar-agar flakes
   Tamari soy sauce
   1 tsp. fresh ginger juice
   Miso-lemon-parsley dressing

Separately blanch the onions, carrots, sweet corn, green peas, and celery. Remove, drain, and mix the vegetables together. Place the vegetables in a shallow casserole dish.

   Place the kombu dashi and agar-agar flakes in a pot. Bring to a boil. Stir frequently to dissolve the flakes. Reduce the flame to low and simmer for 2 to 3 minutes. Add several drops of tamari soy sauce, to mildly season, but not enough to turn the liquid dark. Add the ginger juice and mix. Remove from the flame, and pour the hot liquid over the vegetables. Allow to sit in a cool place or refrigerate until jelled. Slice and serve with miso-lemon-parsley dressing.

Puréed Squash Aspic

   3 cups water or kombu dashi
   5–6 Tbsp. agar-agar flakes
   Pinch of sea salt
   4 cups buttercup or other hard winter squash, sliced and cut into cubes
   Chopped parsley for garnish
   Any miso- or tamari-based dressing (optional)

Place the water and agar-agar flakes in a pot. Add the pinch of sea salt. Stir frequently to dissolve the flakes. Bring to a boil. Add the squash, reduce the flame to medium-low and simmer until soft. Pour the squash and liquid into a hand food mill, and purée until creamy and smooth. Pour the hot purée into a shallow casserole dish. Allow to sit in a cool place or refrigerate until jelled. Garnish with chopped parsley. Slice and serve plain or with suggested dressing above.

Variation: Try puréed carrot, broccoli, or cauliflower in place of squash.

Cabbage and Carrot Aspic

   4–5 cups water or kombu dashi
   5–6 Tbsp. agar-agar flakes
   Pinch of sea salt

¹⁄₂ cup raisins, soaked 10 minutes
1 cup apples, washed and sliced into cubes
1 cup carrots, coarsely grated or sliced in thin matchsticks, blanched 1 minute
1 cup cabbage, finely shredded, blanched 1–2 minutes
Miso-apple dressing

Place the water, agar-agar flakes, and sea salt in a saucepan. Stir frequently to dissolve the flakes. Bring to a boil, reduce the flame to medium-low, and simmer for 2 to 3 minutes.

Place the raisins in the bottom of the casserole dish. Pour enough hot liquid over the raisins to just lightly cover them. Allow to sit for several minutes in the refrigerator or freezer until almost jelled.

Set the cubed apples on top of the gelled raisins. Pour more hot liquid over the apples just to cover. Return to the freezer and allow to jell. Place a layer of carrots on top of the jelled apples. Pour hot liquid over, just to cover, and return to the freezer until jelled.

Next, layer the shredded cabbage on top of the jelled carrots, and pour the remaining hot liquid over the cabbage until completely covered. Return to the freezer or refrigerator and let sit for several more minutes until the aspic is completely jelled. When completely jelled, slice and serve with a miso-apple dressing.

Quick Pickles

Quick pickles require less time, pressure, and salt than pickles that are fermented for longer periods. They have more yin, lighter energy than long-term pickles. By slicing the vegetables very thinly, we speed up the pickling process and reduce the length of time it takes for fermentation to begin. Quick pickles are good for those who wish to reduce their intake of salt, and add a nice, light touch to meals.

Natural pickling agents such as sea salt, tamari soy sauce, and umeboshi plum, or brown rice, umeboshi, or high-quality apple cider vinegar can be used to make quick pickles. Natural sweeteners such as mirin, barley malt, or rice syrup can also be added for a sweeter flavor.

Pickles can be served individually with meals or mixed in with boiled or raw salads. You can also arrange several varieties on a platter and serve them with meals.

Tamari Soy Sauce-Rutabaga Pickles

2 cups rutabaga, sliced in very thin bite-size pieces
1–1¹⁄₂ cups water
¹⁄₂ cup tamari soy sauce

Place all ingredients in a clean bowl or glass jar, making sure that the rutabaga slices are completely covered by the tamari soy sauce-water solution. Let sit for 2 to 4 hours or up to 4 to 5 days. The longer the pickles sit, the saltier they become. If too salty, rinse them quickly under cold water before serving. These pickles will keep for several days if refrigerated.

Tamari Soy Sauce-Onion Pickles

> 2 cups onions, sliced in very thin half-moons, blanched 30 seconds, and drained
> ½ cup shiitake mushrooms, soaked 10 minutes, stemmed, sliced very thin,
>   and simmered 10–15 minutes
> 1 cup water
> ½ cup tamari soy sauce
> 1 Tbsp. sweet brown rice vinegar
> 1–2 Tbsp. barley malt or rice syrup

After the onions and shiitake have drained and cooled, place them in a clean glass jar. Pour the water, tamari soy sauce, vinegar, and sweetener over the vegetables. Cover and shake to mix. Allow to sit 2 to 3 days or up to 1 week. Remove, rinse, and serve.

Variation: Try blanched, whole small onions, cauliflower, broccoli flowerettes, or other vegetables.

Salt-Brine Pickles

> 10–12 cups water
> ¼–⅓ cup sea salt
> 3–4 pickling cucumbers, washed and sliced in quarters
> 1 cup onions, sliced in thick wedges, blanched 30 seconds, rinsed, and drained
> 1 cup broccoli flowerettes
> 1 cup cauliflower flowerettes
> ½ cup carrots, sliced on a thin diagonal
> 3–4 sprigs fresh dill (optional)

Combine the water and sea salt in a pot. Bring to a boil. Reduce the flame to medium-low and simmer until the salt is completely dissolved, stirring occasionally. Remove, set aside, and allow to cool completely.

Place the vegetables in a large glass jar or ceramic crock. Pour the cooled salt solution over the vegetables. Cover the jar or crock with a thin layer of clean cotton cheesecloth, and allow to sit for 2 to 4 days. Cover and refrigerate for another 1 to 3 days. These pickles will keep for about a month in the refrigerator.

Variation: Try daikon slices, red radishes, cabbage, or even watermelon rind.

Daikon-Sauerkraut Pickles

> 2 cups daikon, sliced in thin rounds
> 1 cup naturally prepared sauerkraut
> 1 cup sauerkraut juice
> 1 cup water

Place the daikon and sauerkraut in a clean glass jar. Cover with water and sauerkraut juice. Shake to mix. Cover the jar with clean, cotton cheesecloth, and let sit for 3 days or up to a week (refrigerate after third day). These pickles will keep for about a month in the refrigerator.

Umeboshi Pickles

> 2 cups red radishes, sliced in thin rounds
> 1 cup red radish greens, sliced in 1-inch lengths
> 2 Tbsp. umeboshi vinegar

Place all ingredients in a pickle press and mix thoroughly. Cover and apply pressure. Let sit for 2 to 3 days. Remove, rinse, and serve.

Daikon-Lemon Pickles

> 2 cups daikon, sliced in thin matchsticks
> 4–5 thick matchstick-size pieces of lemon rind
> Sea salt

Place the daikon and lemon in a pickle press. Sprinkle a small amount of sea salt on the daikon for a mild salt flavor (taste a piece of daikon to test for saltiness). Mix well. Place the cover on the press, and screw the plate down to apply pressure. Let sit for 3 to 4 hours. Remove the lemon rind and discard. Keep in a cool place for 3 to 4 days. Remove the pickles from the press to refrigerate. These pickles will keep for several days.

Turnip-Kombu Pickles

> 2–3 cups turnips, washed, halved, and sliced in paper-thin half-moons
> Sea salt
> 1 strip kombu, 4–6 inches long, soaked 3–5 minutes, sliced in very thin matchsticks

Place the turnips in a bowl. Sprinkle with a small amount of sea salt for a mild salt flavor. Add the kombu and mix thoroughly. Place in a pickle press, cover, apply pressure, and allow to sit for 2 to 3 days. Remove from the press and refrigerate. These pickles will keep for several days.

Miso-Cucumber Pickles

> **1–2 cucumbers, sliced in $\frac{1}{8}$–$\frac{1}{4}$-inch rounds**
> **Barley miso**

Place the cucumbers in a clean glass jar and completely cover them with miso. Let sit for 1 to 2 days. Remove and serve. If too salty, rinse under cold water. Save the miso and use again.

Chapter 8

Bean and Tofu Salads

Bean salads can be served warm, at room temperature, or slightly chilled. The rich flavors and soft textures of beans and bean products blend very well with the more crispy texture of raw vegetables. A variety of beans can be used in making salads and aspics, as can soy foods such as tofu, tempeh, and natto. Beans and bean products add protein to the diet without the cholesterol and saturated fat contained in animal foods.

Cooking Beans

It is best to soak beans several hours or overnight before cooking. Beans can be soaked in either cold or warm water. Warm water produces a softer-textured bean dish, and reduces slightly the length of time needed for cooking. Cold water gives beans a firmer texture, which is often desirable in salads, but lengthens the amount of time needed for cooking. If you use warm water, the beans need to be soaked for about 4 to 6 hours, while most beans need to be soaked for 6 to 8 hours or overnight if you use cold water. Soft beans such as green and red lentils and split peas need not be soaked.

Another important procedure in cooking beans is to add kombu at the beginning. Kombu contains valuable minerals that help bring out the naturally sweet, rich flavor of the beans. Kombu also makes beans easier to digest and shortens the amount of time needed to cook them. A strip of kombu, 1 or 2 inches wide is usually sufficient for a cup of dried beans. Simply take a clean damp sponge and brush the kombu off before adding it to the beans.

Boiling is the method of cooking used most often for beans, followed by pressure-cooking. Long, slow boiling produces beans that are soft, sweet, and easy to digest. Pressure-cooking can be used on occasion when time is a concern. Pressure-cooking makes beans somewhat firmer and less sweet than boiling does. Below are instructions for cooking beans with these methods.

1. Boiling—Soak beans as instructed above. Place kombu in the pot and add the beans. Add cold water (not the soaking water, except when using azuki beans or black soybeans) to just cover the beans. Cover, bring to a boil, reduce the flame to medium-low, and simmer until about 80 percent done. Add sea salt (1/8 to 1/4 teaspoon per cup of dried beans), and simmer another 10 to 15 minutes.

As they cook, the beans will absorb water and expand. Therefore, it is necessary to add more water from time to time. Add just enough water to cover the beans each time. Check the beans several times while cooking to make sure there is enough water in the pot to prevent them from burning. Once you add sea salt or seasoning such as tamari soy sauce, it is unnecessary to add more water. Continue to simmer until the beans are completely done.

If you are making a salad, remove the beans, and let them drain and cool. The cooking water can be saved and used in soups. If you are making a bean aspic, the cooking water can be used as a part of the water called for in the recipe.

2. Pressure-cooking—Soak the beans as indicated above. Then place kombu in the bottom of the pressure cooker, and set the beans on top. Add water, cover, and bring up to pressure. Reduce the flame to medium-low, and cook for the length of time indicated in the chart below.

When the beans have finished cooking, turn off the flame, remove the pressure cooker from the burner, and allow the pressure to come down naturally. Remove the cover. Season with sea salt (about 1/8 teaspoon per cup of dried beans) and then simmer over a low flame for about 10 to 15 minutes. Place the beans in a colander, drain, and allow to cool. If you are preparing an aspic, use the cooking water and follow the instructions in the recipe.

Approximate Cooking Times for Beans (per 1 cup dried beans)

Beans	Boiling		Pressure-cooking	
	Water (cup)	Time (hours)	Water (cup)	Time (hours)
Azuki	3–3½	2½	2–2½	¾
Lentils	3–3½	1¼	—	—
Kidney beans	3–3½	2½	2–2½	1
Chick-peas	3–4	4	2–2½	1½

Beans	Boiling		Pressure-cooking	
	Water (cup)	Time (hours)	Water (cup)	Time (hours)
Pinto beans	3–3½	3	2–2½	1–1¼
Soybeans	3–3½	3	2–2½	1
Black soybeans	3–3½	3–3½	—	—
Split peas	3–3½	1½	—	—
Red lentils	3–3½	1½	—	—
Navy beans	3–3½	2½	2–2½	¾
Northern beans	3–3½	2½	2–2½	1
Lima beans	3–3½	2–3	2–2½	1
Black turtle beans	3–3½	2½	2–2½	¾

Bean Salads

Chick-pea-Vegetable Salad

2 cups chick-peas, cooked and drained
¼ cup red onion, halved and sliced in thin half-rings
¼ cup carrots, diced or sliced in matchsticks, and blanched sevral seconds
¼ cup celery, sliced on a thin diagonal and blanched 30 seconds
¼ cup cucumber, sliced in rounds and then matchsticks
1 Tbsp. chopped parsley
Several fresh lettuce leaves, washed
Umeboshi-scallion, or chive dressing

Place all ingredients except the lettuce and dressing in a bowl and mix well. Line a bowl or platter with the lettuce leaves. Just before serving, mix in the dressing, and place the salad on top of the bed of lettuce.

Three Bean Salad

1 cup kidney beans, cooked and drained
2 cups green string beans, stemmed, boiled 2–3 minutes or until tender, and sliced in 1–2-inch lengths
1 cup yellow wax beans, stemmed, boiled 2–3 minutes or until tender, and sliced in 1–2-inch lengths
2 tsp. finely minced onion
Umeboshi-parsley, scallion, or chive dressing

Place the beans and onion in a bowl and mix well. Mix in the dressing several minutes before serving to marinate. Place in a serving dish. Garnish and serve.

Variation: Try cooked chick-peas or pinto beans in addition to, or in place of, kidney beans.

Kidney Bean-Dandelion Salad

2–3 cups kidney beans, cooked and drained
1 cup fresh dandelion greens, washed, sliced, blanched 30 seconds, drained, and
   sautéed 1–2 minutes in dark sesame oil and seasoned with a few drops of
   tamari soy sauce
1 cup yellow wax beans, stemmed, boiled 2–3 minutes or until tender, and sliced
   in 1–2-inch lengths
Umeboshi dressing

Combine all ingredients and place in a serving bowl.

Navy Bean Salad

2–3 cups navy beans, cooked and drained
½ cup sweet corn, removed from cob and boiled 1 minute
¼ cup onion, diced, blanched several seconds or left raw
¼ cup carrots, diced, blanched 1 minute
Several lettuce leaves, washed
Parsley sprigs for garnish
Brown rice vinegar-tamari soy sauce dressing

Place the beans, corn, onion, and carrots in a bowl and mix. Line a bowl with
the lettuce leaves. Place the bean-salad mixture on top of the leaves. Garnish with
several sprigs of parsley. Spoon the dressing over individual servings of salad.

Soybean Relish

1–1½ cups soybeans, washed and dry-roasted
1 strip kombu, 3–4 inches long, soaked and diced
Water
Dark sesame oil
¼ cup burdock, diced
¼ cup fresh lotus root, diced
½ cup carrots, diced
Puréed barley miso
¼–⅓ tsp. fresh ginger juice
1 Tbsp. chopped chives or scallions

Place the kombu in a pressure cooker and set the beans on top. Add enough water
to almost cover. Cover the cooker and bring up to pressure. Reduce the flame to
medium-low, and cook for 35 to 40 minutes. Remove from the flame and allow
the pressure to come down. Remove and drain.

   Brush a small amount of dark sesame oil in a skillet and heat it up. Add the
burdock, and sauté for 1 minute. Add the lotus root, and sauté for 1 minute. Next,
add the carrots, and sauté together with the burdock and lotus root for several
minutes, until tender, stirring often to evenly sauté.

   Add the soybeans and a small amount of puréed barley miso for a mild salt taste. Cover, reduce the flame to medium-low, and simmer for 2 to 3 minutes. Add the fresh ginger juice and chopped chives or scallions. Leave the cover off, mix, and sauté until all liquid is gone. Remove and place in a serving dish.

If mildly seasoned, this can be served as a salad. However, if heavily seasoned with miso, it is better to use it in small amounts as a condiment with whole grain or other dishes.

Green Beans with Sesame Seed Dressing

> **3–4 cups green string beans, stemmed, boiled 2–3 minutes or until tender, and sliced in 3-inch lengths**
> **½ cup tan sesame seeds, dry-roasted**
> **Tamari soy sauce**
> **¼ cup water or kombu dashi**

Place the sesame seeds in a suribachi and grind until half-crushed. Add several drops of tamari soy sauce and the water or dashi. Grind to mix well. Place the green beans in the sesame mixture, and mix well. Remove and place in a serving dish.

Variation: Combine a small amount of white miso with the water or dashi and simmer on low heat until thick. Then mix in with the ground sesame seeds. Grind to a smooth paste. Add the string beans and mix well.

Mung Bean Sprout Salad

> **2–3 cups fresh mung bean sprouts, boiled 2–3 minutes and drained**
> **Tamari-brown rice vinegar dressing**

Place the sprouts in individual dishes, and spoon the dressing over while serving.

Variation: Try tamari soy sauce-ginger dressing, or miso-mustard dressing.

Tofu and Tempeh Salads ——————————

Tofu Salad

> **2 cakes (2 lbs.) fresh, firm-style tofu, cubed**
> **Chopped scallions for garnish**
> **Bonito flakes for garnish (optional)**
> **Tamari-ginger dressing**

Place the cubed tofu in individual serving dishes. Sprinkle a few chopped scallions and a small amount of bonito flakes over the tofu. Spoon the dressing over the garnished tofu when served.

Individuals with health problems may want to blanch the tofu cubes for 1 minute, drain, and cool before garnishing and serving.

Tofu-Vegetable Salad

> ½ cup carrot, diced, blanched 1 minute, and drained
> ½ cup celery, diced
> ¼ cup red onion, diced
> Tofu-umeboshi-tahini dressing
> Lettuce leaves, washed
> Chopped parsley for garnish

Place the carrots, celery, red onion, and tofu dressing in a bowl and mix well. Arrange lettuce leaves in individual serving dishes. Spoon the salad onto the leaves. Garnish each serving with a small amount of chopped parsley.

Tempeh Salad #1

> 2 cups tempeh, cubed, simmered in water, a little tamari soy sauce, and a slice of
>   ginger for 20 minutes (remove and drain)
> 2 cups leeks, washed, sliced on a thin diagonal, boiled 1–2 minutes, and drained
> ½ cup carrots, sliced in thin matchsticks, blanched 30 seconds, and drained
> Umeboshi-parsley dressing or tamari-ginger dressing

Combine the tempeh, leeks, and carrots. Place in individual serving dishes. Spoon one of the above dressings over the salad as served.

Variation: Try deep-frying the tempeh cubes until golden brown before simmering, for a richer flavor.

Tempeh Salad #2

> 2 cups tempeh, boiled in a little water and tamari soy sauce for 15–20 minutes,
>   drained, and chopped very finely
> ½ cup celery, diced
> ¼ cup onion, minced
> Prepared tofu mayonnaise
> Lettuce leaves, washed
> Chopped parsley for garnish

Place the tempeh, celery, and onion in a bowl. Add a small amount of prepared tofu mayonnaise, or creamy tofu dressing, and mix well.

Arrange a fresh lettuce leaf in each serving dish, and spoon the salad onto the leaf. Garnish with chopped parsley and serve.

Notes: This salad can be used as a filler for whole-grain-bread sandwiches.

Natto Salads and Side Dishes

Natto with Mustard

>2 containers of natto (1½–2 cups)
>1 tsp. fresh miso mustard or yellow mustard
>2 Tbsp. chopped scallions or chives
>Tamari soy sauce
>Parsley sprigs for garnish

Place the natto, mustard, chopped scallions, and a few drops of tamari soy sauce in a bowl. Mix well. Place the natto in individual serving dishes and garnish with a small sprig of parsley on the side of each dish.

Natto with Grated Daikon

>2 containers of natto (1½–2 cups)
>2–3 Tbsp. fresh grated daikon
>2 Tbsp. chopped chives or scallions
>Tamari soy sauce
>Several red-radish rounds for garnish

Place the natto, daikon, chives or scallions, and a few drops of tamari soy sauce in a bowl. Mix well. Spoon the natto into individual serving dishes and garnish each with 1 to 2 rounds of red radish.

Bean Aspics

Azuki Bean-Raisin Aspic

>1 cup azuki beans, washed and soaked 6–8 hours
>1 strip kombu, 3–4 inches, soaked and diced
>¼ cup raisins
>4–5 cups water
>¼–½ tsp. sea salt
>5–6 Tbsp. agar-agar flakes
>2 lemon twists for garnish
>2 parsley sprigs for garnish

Place the kombu, azuki beans, and raisins in a pot. Add the water. Bring to a boil. Reduce the flame to medium-low, cover, and simmer until the beans are almost done (about 2 hours). Season with sea salt, and thoroughly mix in the agar-agar flakes to properly dissolve them. Simmer, uncovered, another 10 minutes or so. Pour into individual serving dishes or a large glass baking dish. Refrigerate until jelled. Garnish with lemon twists and parsley sprigs. Slice and serve chilled.

Variation: For a smoother consistency, purée the azuki beans in a hand food mill after cooking, and then refrigerate until jelled.

Split Pea Aspic

> 1 cup green split peas, washed
> ¼ cup wakame, soaked and finely chopped
> ½ cup onion, grated
> 4–5 cups water
> ¼–½ tsp. sea salt
> 5–6 Tbsp. agar-agar flakes
> ¼ cup carrot (either raw or blanched for 30 seconds), sliced into flowers, maple
>   leaves, or pinwheels for garnish

Place the wakame, onion, and split peas in a pot. Add the water, and bring to a boil. Reduce the flame to medium-low, cover, and simmer about 1 to 1 1/2 hours or until very smooth and creamy. Add the sea salt and agar-agar flakes, stirring thoroughly to mix in and properly dissolve. Simmer for another 10 minutes or so.

Remove and place in a glass baking dish or shallow casserole dish. Refrigerate until about half jelled. Garnish the top of the aspic with the carrot flowers, maple leaves, or pinwheels. Allow to sit until completely jelled. Slice and serve.

Lentil Aspic

> 1 cup lentils, washed
> 1 strip kombu, 3–4 inches long, soaked and diced
> 1 cup onion, diced
> ½ cup carrot, diced
> ½ cup celery, diced
> 4–5 cups water
> ¼–½ tsp. sea salt
> 5–6 Tbsp. agar-agar flakes
> 1 Tbsp. chopped parsley

Place the kombu, onion, carrot, celery, lentils, and water in a pot. Cover and bring to a boil. Reduce the flame to medium-low, and simmer for 1 to 1 1/2 hours, until soft and creamy. Add the sea salt and agar-agar flakes, thoroughly mixing in until completely dissolved. Simmer for another 10 to 15 minutes. Remove and place in a casserole or baking dish. Refrigerate until jelled. Garnish with chopped parsley, slice, and serve.

Puréed Chick-pea Aspic

> 1 cup chick-peas, washed and soaked 6–8 hours
> 1 strip kombu, 3–4 inches long, soaked and diced
> 4–5 cups water
> ¼–½ tsp. sea salt

5–6 Tbsp. agar-agar flakes
$\frac{1}{2}$ **cup cucumbers, sliced in thin rounds and then matchsticks**
$\frac{1}{2}$ **cup carrots, sliced in thin matchsticks**
$\frac{1}{4}$ **cup scallions or chives, finely chopped**
Tamari-ginger dressing
$\frac{1}{2}$ **cup croutons**

Place the kombu, chick-peas, and water in a pressure cooker. Cover, and bring up to pressure. Reduce the flame to medium-low, and simmer for 1 1/2 hours. Remove from the flame and allow the pressure to come down. Remove the cover and purée the chick-peas, with the cooking water, in a hand food mill until smooth.

Place the purée in a pot, and add the sea salt and agar-agar flakes. Stir constantly until the flakes are completely dissolved. Simmer for another 10 to 15 minutes. Remove and pour into a shallow casserole or baking dish. Refrigerate until jelled. Slice and place in individual serving dishes.

While the beans are cooking, place the cucumbers, carrots, and scallions or chives in a bowl. Pour the tamari-ginger dressing over the vegetables. Allow to marinate for 15 to 20 minutes.

Place a tablespoon or so of marinated vegetables, a small amount of the dressing, and several croutons on top of each serving. Serve chilled.

Chapter 9

Sea-vegetable Salads

Sea vegetables, although new to many people today, have been used in traditional diets for centuries. In cultures throughout the world, people relied on sea vegetables as a source of iron, calcium, iodine, and other essential minerals. Edible plants from the sea were traditionally harvested by coastal people in Europe, Asia, Africa, Australia, and other parts of the world. They were used as snacks, in making porridges, breads, jellies, and preserves, as well as ingredients in natural shampoos and cosmetics.

Sea vegetables are an important part of a healthful diet. They can be used in soups, grain, vegetable, and bean dishes, and in desserts and kantens.

Sea-vegetable salads and aspics are especially good during the summer, or in warmer climates, as they are light and easy to digest, and supply minerals that are lost through perspiration. Because they are naturally dried and store easily, sea vegetables can be used as staples throughout the year.

Hundreds of edible sea vegetables are available throughout the world. Those used most frequently in macrobiotic cooking are hijiki, wakame, arame, kombu, nori, dulse, sea palm, and agar-agar.

Washing Sea Vegetables

It is important to wash sea vegetables properly before you soak and cook them. Washing removes sand, dust, small stones, and occasional small shells.

Before washing, place the sea vegetable on a plate, a handful at a time, and sort out any stones, shells, or very hard clumps, and discard them. Next, place the sea vegetable in a bowl and cover with cold water, and swish it around quickly with your hands. Pour off the water. Repeat once or twice. Now place the sea vegetable in a colander or strainer and briefly run under cold water to remove any remaining dust. This rinsing process can be used for hijiki, arame, wakame, unprocessed wild nori (not sheet nori or flakes), sea palm, and dulse. Sheet nori and nori flakes do not require washing, nor does agar-agar. Kombu can be simply dusted off by running a clean, damp sponge along both sides of it.

Soaking Sea Vegetables

After washing, place the sea vegetable in a bowl, cover with cold water, and soak for 3 to 5 minutes. It is now ready for slicing. Arame does not need to be soaked before slicing. This sea vegetable has a very soft texture and is pre-shredded. It loses much of its sweet flavor and nutrients if it is soaked. Sheet nori, nori flakes, and agar-agar flakes and powder do not require soaking before using (bars of agar-agar do require soaking, however). After your sea vegetable has been washed and soaked, it is now ready to slice and cook.

Salads and Aspics ————————————————

Hijiki Salad

> 2 cups hijiki, washed, soaked, and sliced
> Water
> ½ cup onions, sliced in thick half-moons
> ½ cup sweet corn, removed from the cob
> 1 cup Chinese cabbage, sliced in 1–2-inch pieces
> ½ cup broccoli, flowerettes
> ¼ cup red radish, sliced in thin rounds
> Lettuce leaves
> Tofu dressing

Place the hijiki in a pot and add water to half-cover. Bring to a boil, reduce the flame to medium-low, cover, and simmer for 20 to 30 minutes. Remove the hijiki and place in a colander or strainer. Rinse quickly under cold water.

While the hijiki is cooking, blanch the vegetables except lettuce leaves, separately, in boiling water until tender but still slightly crisp and brightly colored. Remove, rinse under cold water, and drain each vegetable after cooking.

Line a serving bowl with fresh lettuce leaves. Either mix the vegetables together with the hijiki in a bowl, and then place on the bed of lettuce, or attractively arrange the vegetables in a separate area of the serving bowl so that they surround the hijiki.

You may serve the tofu dressing separately in a small bowl, spooning it over individual servings, or mix it in with the salad before placing on the bed of lettuce.

Wakame-Cucumber Salad

> 1 cup wakame, washed, soaked, and sliced
> Water
> 1 cup cucumber, skin removed and sliced in thin rounds
> 1 cup apple, cored, and sliced in thin half-moons or small chunks
> Miso-lemon or miso-vinegar dressing

Place the wakame in a pot. Add enough water to half cover. Bring to a boil, reduce the flame to medium-low, cover, and simmer for 5 to 10 minutes. Remove, rinse quickly under cold water, and drain.

Mix the wakame, cucumber, and apple together in a bowl. Pour the dressing over the salad, and let sit for 30 minutes or so. Drain off any excess liquid, and place in a serving bowl.

Variation: Try slices of tangerine or orange in place of apples for a different flavor and appearance.

Pressed Wakame and Lettuce Salad

> 1 cup wakame, washed, soaked, sliced, and simmered 5–10 minutes (remove, rinse, and drain)
> 2 cups lettuce, washed and shredded or torn into bite-size pieces
> $\frac{1}{4}$ cup red radish, sliced in thin rounds
> $\frac{1}{4}$ cup celery, sliced on a thin diagonal
> $\frac{1}{4}$ cup cucumber, sliced in quarters and then on a thin diagonal
> $\frac{1}{2}$ tsp. sea salt
> 1–2 Tbsp. brown rice vinegar, or fresh lemon or orange juice

Place all ingredients in a mixing bowl and combine well. Next, place the salad mixture in a pickle press. Place the top on the press, screw the pressure plate down to apply pressure, and let sit for 1 to 1 1/2 hours. Remove, squeeze out any excess liquid, and if too salty, rinse quickly under cold water before serving. Place in a serving bowl.

Variation: Try very finely shredded cabbage or Chinese cabbage in place of lettuce.

Wakame with Tofu Dressing

> 2 cups wakame, washed, soaked, sliced, and simmered 5–10 minutes (remove, quickly rinse, and drain)
> 1 cup cucumber slices, pressed in salt 1 hour
> Tofu-umeboshi dressing

¼ cup carrots, sliced in very thin flower or pinwheel shapes

Place the wakame and cucumbers in a bowl. Mix well. Mix the tofu dressing in just before serving. Place in a serving bowl and garnish with the carrot flowers or pinwheels.

Wakame-Daikon-Carrot Salad

1 cup wakame, washed, soaked, sliced, and simmered 5–10 minutes
   (remove, quickly rinse, and drain)
1 cup daikon, sliced in thin matchsticks and blanched 1 minute
½ cup carrot, sliced in thin matchsticks and blanched 1 minute
¼ cup celery, sliced on a thin diagonal and blanched 1 minute
Tamari soy sauce-vinegar-ginger dressing

Place the wakame and vegetables in a bowl and mix. Pour the dressing over the salad and marinate for about 15 minutes. Remove, drain, and place in a serving bowl.

Arame-Corn Salad

1 cup arame, washed, drained, sliced, and simmered 5–10 minutes
   (remove, quickly rinse, and drain)
1 cup sweet corn, removed from cob, boiled 1–2 minutes, and drained
1 cup snow peas, stringed, sliced in half, and blanched 1 minute
Creamy tofu dressing

Place all ingredients together in a bowl and mix. Place in a serving bowl and garnish. Instead of mixing the dressing in with the salad, you may serve it separately, spooning it over each serving.

Dulse Salad

½ cup dulse, washed, soaked, sliced, and simmered 3–5 minutes
   (remove, quickly rinse, and drain)
1 cup Chinese cabbage, sliced in 1-inch pieces and blanched 1 minute
½ cup daikon, sliced in matchsticks and boiled 1 minute
½ cup carrot, sliced in matchsticks and boiled 1 minute
¼ cup onion, sliced in thin half-moons and blanched 45 seconds
¼ cup celery, sliced on a thin diagonal and boiled 1 minute
Umeboshi-sesame dressing

Place the dulse and vegetables in a bowl and mix. Just before serving, pour the dressing over the salad and mix well. Place in a serving bowl.

Dulse-Cucumber Salad

> 1 cup dulse, washed, soaked, sliced, and simmered 3–5 minutes
>   (remove, quickly rinse, and drain)
> 2 cups cucumbers (score the skin of the cucumber with a fork and slice
>   into thin rounds)
> Umeboshi-sesame seed or umeboshi-tahini dressing

Place the dulse and cucumbers in a bowl and mix. Just before serving, mix in the dressing and place in a serving bowl.

Dulse-Lettuce Salad

> 1 cup dulse, washed, soaked, sliced, and simmered 3–5 minutes
>   (remove, quickly rinse, and drain)
> 2 cups romaine lettuce, torn in bite-size pieces
> 1 cup apple, cored and sliced in bite-size pieces
> Brown rice vinegar-oil dressing

Place the dulse, romaine lettuce, and apples in a bowl and mix. Just before serving, pour the dressing over the salad, toss, and place in a serving bowl.

Nori-Vegetable Sushi

> 4–5 sheets nori, toasted
> 2 bunches watercress (or 1 bunch turnip or mustard greens), washed
> Water
> Several strips of pickled shiso leaves (packed with umeboshi plums)
> ¼ cup tan sesame seeds, roasted

Place about an inch of water in a pot and bring to a boil. Add the whole watercress (or turnip or mustard greens). Blanch the watercress for about 45 seconds, or if using turnip or mustard greens, cover and boil 1 to 2 minutes. Remove, quickly rinse under cold water to stop the cooking action, and allow to drain. Squeeze out excess liquid.

Place a sheet of toasted nori on a bamboo sushi mat. Lay the whole, uncut greens across the entire width of the sheet of nori, covering all but 1 inch at the bottom and about 2 to 3 inches at the top of the sheet. Lay several strips of shiso leaves in a straight line across the width of the greens about 2 inches from the bottom. Sprinkle roasted sesame seeds on top of the shiso leaves.

Roll up the sushi in the same manner as for rice sushi (see Chapter 5). When the greens are completely rolled up in the nori, wrap the sushi mat around the roll, and squeeze gently but firmly to remove excess liquid. Slice immediately after rolling. Do not wet your knife when cutting as you do when making rice sushi, as this will cause the nori to become too wet and fall apart. After slicing the sushi, arrange on a serving platter, garnish, and serve.

Variations: Try using daikon greens or kale in place of the greens in this recipe. You may also use sauerkraut or pickles in place of shiso leaves, or roasted and chopped sunflower or pumpkin seeds in place of the sesame seeds. You may also place strips of cooked carrots on top of the greens before rolling up, giving a nice orange center to the sushi.

Grated Daikon with Toasted Nori Strips

Although this is not actually a salad, it is a delicious side dish when served with a meal containing fish, seafood, or other item that is high in oil. The daikon aids in the digestion of these foods.

> **1 cup freshly grated daikon**
> **½ sheet nori, toasted and sliced in thin strips**
> **Tamari soy sauce**

Place the daikon in a serving bowl. Sprinkle several drops of tamari soy sauce in the center of the daikon. Sprinkle several nori strips over the daikon as you serve it.

Green Nori Flakes

Green nori flakes can be sprinkled over any grain, noodle or vegetable salad instead of, or in combination with, a dressing. They add a nice pale green color, iron and other minerals, and a slightly different flavor to your salads.

Kombu

Kombu is used most often in preparing grains, soups, and bean and vegetable dishes. It can also be cooked until soft, and used in vegetable salads or soaked and used in making quick root-vegetable pickles. See Chapter 7 for specific recipes.

Kombu-Carrot Rolls

> **2 wide strips kombu, 10–12 inches long, washed and soaked**
> **4 medium-sized carrots, 6–8 inches long, washed**
> **10–12 strips *kanpyo* (dried edible gourd strips), 3 inches long, soaked 3–5 minutes**
> **Water**
> **Tamari soy sauce**
> **Any tamari- or umeboshi-based dressing**

Slice the strips of kombu in half, so that each strip is now about 5 to 6 inches long. Place one of these strips on a cutting board and place a carrot on top of it. Roll the carrot up inside the kombu as tightly as possible, so that it is completely covered.

Take 3 strips of the kanpyo and tie them around both ends and around the middle of each roll. Repeat until the kombu and carrots are used up.

Place the kombu-carrot rolls in a pressure cooker and add about 1/4 to 1/2 inch of water and several drops of tamari soy sauce. Cover the cooker, bring to pressure, reduce the flame to medium-low, and cook for 3 to 5 minutes. Allow the pressure to come down. Remove the kombu-carrot rolls and place on a cutting surface. Slice each roll into 3 equal-size pieces, so that each piece is still tied together with the kanpyo. Arrange on a serving platter so that each roll stands on end or lies on its side.

When the rolls are served, each person can spoon dressing over them before eating.

Sweet Sea Palm Salad

> 2 cups sea palm, washed, soaked, sliced in 2-inch-long pieces, and steamed several
>   minutes until tender (remove, quickly rinse, and drain)
> 1–2 Tbsp. brown rice vinegar
> 2 Tbsp. brown rice syrup
> Tamari soy sauce
> 1 Tbsp. tan sesame seeds, roasted

Mix the brown rice vinegar, rice syrup, and several drops of tamari soy sauce together. Pour over the sea palm and mix. Place in a serving dish. Sprinkle the roasted sesame seeds over the salad and serve.

Agar-agar Squares with Miso-Apple Dressing

> 4 cups water
> 1 strip kombu, 3–4 inches long, washed
> 4–5 Tbsp. agar-agar flakes
> Miso-apple dressing
> Chopped parsley for garnish

Place the water, kombu, and agar-agar flakes in a pot. Bring to a boil, stirring to dissolve the flakes. Reduce the flame to medium-low, and simmer for 3 to 5 minutes. Remove the kombu and set aside for future use.

Place the liquid in a bowl and refrigerate until jelled. Slice the agar-agar or clear kanten into 2-inch squares. Place in individual serving dishes and spoon the dressing over it. Garnish each with a small amount of chopped parsley.

Chapter 10

Fruit Salads and Kanten

Fruits have a refreshing, cooling energy that is especially nice on warm summer days. They can be used to complement and make balance for a warming meal, or to help relax our condition. Fresh raw fruit is best eaten mostly in warmer seasons, but can be enjoyed on occasion in other seasons by those in good health. Cooked- or dried-fruit desserts, including puddings, custards, compotes, kantens, and others can also be enjoyed throughout the year, on average, several times per week.

A wide variety of seasonal fruits can be used in fresh salads. Recommended temperate-climate fruits include honeydew melon, cantaloupe, watermelon, strawberries, raspberries, blackberries, blueberries, and other berries, peaches, apricots, plums, grapes, nectarines, and of course apples and pears. In general, tropical fruits are not recommended for regular use in a temperate climate. Citrus fruits, such as lemons or tangerines, can be used from time to time by those in good health as a garnish or occasionally in making salads.

Organic, unsprayed fruit is best for health. If high-quality natural fruit is not available, as much as possible try to select fruit that is minimally sprayed and unwaxed.

It is important to wash fruit thoroughly before using it. If the fruit is waxed, it is best to remove the skin for optimum flavor and health.

Fruit Salads —————————

Spring-Summer Fruit Salad

    1 cup watermelon balls
    1 cup cantaloupe, cubed
    1 cup honeydew melon, cubed
    ½ cup strawberries, halved
    ½ cup seedless grapes
    ¼ cup blueberries
    Pinch of sea salt

Place all fruit in a bowl and sprinkle a small amount of sea salt over it. Mix well. Place in a serving bowl as is, or on a bed of fresh lettuce leaves, or in individual fruit cups. Serve at room temperature or slightly chilled.

Autumn-Winter Fruit Salad

    1 cup red apples, cored and sliced
    1 cup green apples, cored and sliced
    1 cup pears, cored and sliced
    1 cup red or green seedless grapes
    ¼ cup raisins
    Pinch of sea salt

Place all fruit in a bowl and sprinkle a small amount of sea salt over it. Mix well. Place in a serving bowl or in individual fruit cups. Serve at room temperature.

Glazed Peaches with Tofu Cheese Slices

    4–5 peaches, halved and pits removed
    1 cup water or apple juice
    Pinch of sea salt
    1 Tbsp. kuzu, diluted
    Fresh lettuce leaves, washed
    8–10 slices tofu cheese

Place the peaches, water or apple juice, and sea salt in a saucepan. Cover, bring to a boil, reduce the flame to low, and simmer several minutes until the peaches are soft and tender. Remove the peaches. Thicken the cooking liquid with the diluted kuzu, stirring constantly to prevent lumping. When the liquid forms a thick sauce and is translucent, remove from the flame.

Place a lettuce leaf on individual dessert plates. Set two peach halves on each leaf. Spoon several tablespoons of sauce over the peaches. Set two slices of tofu cheese next to the peaches on the side of each plate. Serve warm, at room temperature, or slightly chilled, depending on the season.

Fresh Strawberries in Sauce

> **2 pints fresh strawberries, washed, stems removed, and sliced in half**
> **2 cups apple juice**
> **Pinch of sea salt**
> **2 Tbsp. kuzu, diluted**

Place the strawberries, apple juice, and sea salt in a saucepan and bring to a boil. Cover, reduce the flame to low, and simmer several minutes, until the strawberries are tender. Add the diluted kuzu, stirring constantly to prevent lumping. When the sauce is thick, remove from the flame. Place the strawberries and sauce in individual fruit cups.

Variations:
1. Use other varieties of fruit instead of strawberries.
2. Serve the strawberries over cake or corn bread and use as strawberry shortcake.
3. Make a crunch with roasted oat flakes and nuts, sweetened with barley malt or rice syrup, to sprinkle over the strawberries.

Puddings, Custards, and Compotes ————

Puddings, custards, and compotes can be served warm, at room temperature, or slightly chilled, depending on the season.

Amazaké-Blueberry Pudding

> **1 quart fresh amazaké**
> **1 pint fresh blueberries, washed, stems removed**
> **2–3 Tbsp. kuzu, diluted**

Place the amazaké in a saucepan. Add the diluted kuzu, stirring frequently to prevent lumping. Bring to a boil, reduce the flame to low, and simmer until thick. Add the blueberries to the thickened amazaké and mix in. Simmer 1 to 2 minutes. Remove and place in individual dessert cups or in a serving bowl.

Amazaké-Tangerine Pudding

> **1 quart amazaké**
> **2 cups tangerine sections, seeds removed**
> **2–3 Tbsp. kuzu, diluted**

Prepare as above.

Amazaké-Pear or Apple Pudding

> 1 quart amazaké
> 1 cup pears or apples, cubed
> 2–3 Tbsp. kuzu diluted

Prepare as above, except add the fruit at the beginning, rather than at the end of cooking, as winter fruits are harder and require a longer time to cook.

Brown Rice Pudding

> 1 cup cooked brown rice
> 1 cup cooked sweet brown rice
> 4 cups water or apple juice
> $\frac{1}{4}$ cup raisins
> Pinch of sea salt
> $\frac{1}{2}$ cup dried apples, soaked and sliced
> $\frac{1}{2}$ cup barley malt or rice syrup
> 2 tsp. organic, roasted tahini (optional)
> $\frac{1}{2}$ tsp. cinnamon (optional)

Place the rice, sweet rice, water or apple juice, raisins, sea salt, and dried apples in a pressure cooker. Cover, and bring up to pressure. Reduce the flame to medium-low, and cook for 30 minutes. Remove from the flame and allow the pressure to come down.

Remove the cover. Add the barley malt, tahini, and cinnamon. Mix the ingredients together. Place the rice-pudding mixture in a covered baking dish or casserole. Bake at 375°F. for about 35 to 40 minutes. Remove the cover and bake slightly longer to brown the top of the pudding. Remove and serve warm, at room temperature, or slightly chilled, depending on the time of year.

Lemon Pudding

> 4 cups water or apple juice
> 1–2 Tbsp. agar-agar flakes
> Fresh lemon juice
> Rice syrup
> Pinch of sea salt
> 2 Tbsp. kuzu, diluted
> $\frac{1}{4}$ cup almonds, roasted and chopped for garnish

Place the water or apple juice, agar-agar flakes, and enough lemon juice for a sour flavor, in a saucepan. Add enough rice syrup for a mild sweet flavor, and pinch of sea salt. Bring to a boil, reduce the flame to low, and simmer 1 to 2 minutes. Stir occasionally until the agar-agar flakes have dissolved.

Add the diluted kuzu, stirring constantly to prevent lumping, and simmer until thick. Remove and pour into individual dessert cups. Garnish with the chopped, roasted almonds and allow to set until jelled. Serve at room temperature or slightly chilled.

Variation:: Try freshly squeezed tangerine or orange juice instead of lemon juice, or thicken amazaké with diluted kuzu to make a thick, sweet topping for the lemon pudding.

Tahini Custard

> ½ cup raisins
> 2 cups water
> 3 cups apples, peeled and sliced
> 2 cups apple juice
> Pinch of sea salt
> 2–3 Tbsp. organic, roasted tahini
> 5–6 Tbsp. agar-agar flakes

Soak the raisins in 2 cups of water for 20 minutes. Place the apples, raisins, water, apple juice, sea salt, tahini, and agar-agar flakes in a saucepan. Bring to a boil. Reduce the flame to medium-low, stirring to dissolve the agar-agar flakes.

Simmer for 2 to 3 minutes. Remove and place in a bowl. Refrigerate until almost jelled. Place in a blender and purée until smooth and creamy. Place in individual dessert cups and chill again until completely jelled.

Variation.:: Try other types of fruit in place of apples, or use dried instead of fresh fruit, but soak it first with the raisins, then slice and cook.

Dried Fruit Compote

> 2 cups dried apples
> 1 cup dried apricots
> 3–4 cups water
> ¼ cup raisins
> Pinch of sea salt

Place the apples and apricots in a bowl and cover with the water. Soak for 1 hour, remove, and slice. Place the dried fruit, raisins, soaking water, and sea salt in a pot. Cover and bring to a boil. Reduce the flame to medium-low, and simmer until the fruit is soft and the compote is thick. Remove and place in individual dessert cups. Serve warm, at room temperature, or slightly chilled.

If there is a lot of liquid left over, thicken with a small amount of diluted kuzu.

Kantens ——————————————————————

Kantens are jelled desserts made with a natural jelling ingredient called agar-agar, a translucent, tasteless sea vegetable. Fruit kantens can be prepared year round and served at room temperature or slightly chilled. Either fresh or dried fruit can be used in preparing kantens.

Apple-Pear-Raisin Kanten

> 1 quart apple juice or a mixture of half water and half apple juice
> 1 cup apples, sliced
> 1 cup pears, sliced
> ¼ cup raisins
> Pinch of sea salt
> 4–5 Tbsp. agar-agar flakes

Place all ingredients in a saucepan. Stir to dissolve the agar-agar flakes. Bring to a boil. Reduce the flame to medium-low and simmer for 2 to 3 minutes, or until the fruit is soft. Remove and place in a shallow bowl or individual dessert cups. Refrigerate until jelled. Serve at room temperature or chilled.

Summer Fruit Kanten

> 1 quart apple, strawberry, or grape juice
> Pinch of sea salt
> 4–5 Tbsp. agar-agar flakes
> ½ cup watermelon balls
> ½ cup cantaloupe, cubed
> ½ cup green seedless grapes
> ½ cup blueberries

Place the juice, sea salt, and agar-agar flakes in a saucepan, stirring to dissolve the flakes. Bring to a boil. Reduce the flame and simmer for 2 to 3 minutes.

Place the fruit in a shallow bowl, and pour the hot liquid over it. The hot liquid is sufficient to cook the fruit. Refrigerate until jelled. Serve at room temperature or slightly chilled.

Strawberry Kanten Pie

> *Crust:*
> 1 cup couscous
> 1 cup apple juice
> ¾–1 cup water
> Pinch of sea salt
> *Filling:*
> 1 cup water
> 2 cups apple or strawberry juice
> Pinch of sea salt
> 5–6 Tbsp. agar-agar flakes
> 1 cup fresh strawberries, washed, stemmed, and sliced in half

Wash and then drain the couscous. Place the couscous, apple juice, water, and sea salt in a saucepan. Bring to a boil. Reduce the flame to low, cover, and simmer for 5 to 10 minutes. Remove and place the couscous in a pie plate. Pack the couscous firmly in the pie plate to form a crust, covering the entire bottom and sides of the plate.

To prepare the filling, place water, apple or strawberry juice, sea salt, and agar-agar flakes in a saucepan, and bring to a boil. Stir to dissolve the flakes. Reduce the flame to medium-low, and simmer for 2 to 3 minutes. Allow to sit for 10 to 15 minutes, or until slightly cool. Pour the cooled liquid into the couscous crust. Place the strawberries into the liquid. Refrigerate until jelled. When hardened, slice the pie into sections and serve.

Variation: When the pie has jelled, thicken amazaké with diluted kuzu, and spread it over the jelled pie for a topping.

Dried Fruit Kanten

> 1 cup dried apricots
> ¼ cup raisins
> 4 cups water or apple juice
> Pinch of sea salt
> 4–5 Tbsp. agar-agar flakes

Place the fruit in a bowl and cover with the water or apple juice. Soak for 30 minutes or until soft. Slice the apricots.

Place the fruit, water or apple juice, sea salt, and agar-agar flakes in a pot. Bring to a boil. Reduce the flame to medium-low, and simmer 10 minutes, stirring constantly until the flakes have dissolved. Remove and place in a shallow bowl or individual dessert cups. Refrigerate until jelled. Serve at room temperature or slightly chilled.

Glossary of Utensils

High-quality utensils can make a world of difference in the kitchen, saving time and energy and enhancing the flavor and appearance of your salads. The following utensils are especially helpful in preparing the salads and other dishes in this book. (Most are available at natural food or kitchen speciality stores.)

Bamboo Sushi Mats *(Sudare)*—These bamboo mats are used when making rice, vegetable, or noodle sushi. They are also excellent for covering leftovers, as they allow heat to escape and air to enter, and prevent food from drying out. It is worth having several.

Box Grater—This four-sided box grater offers four grating styles, ranging from very fine to thick and long. Stainless-steel varieties are preferred.

Cookware—Quality stainless-steel cookware is important in preparing salads and other dishes. A variety of pots, pans, and skillets are useful at the beginning. Cast-iron and earthenware cookware can also be used.

Cutting Boards—High-quality wood cutting boards are essential in the kitchen. One can be used for vegetable foods only, and if you eat fish, the other for fish and seafood.

Earthenware Crocks—These come in a variety of sizes and can be used when preparing pickles and pressed salads. Several small or medium-sized crocks are usually sufficient.

Flame Tamer or Deflector—These light-weight metal disks are placed underneath

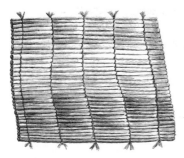

Bamboo Sushi Mat (Sudare)

Earthenware Crocks

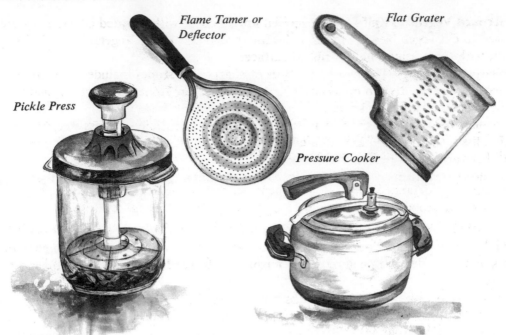

Flame Tamer or Deflector

Flat Grater

Pickle Press

Pressure Cooker

the pressure cooker on the stove to allow even distribution of heat and prevent burning.

Flat Grater—These stainless-steel or porcelain flat graters from Japan are very useful for grating items such as ginger, daikon, or other foods for use as garnishes or in dressings. The stainless-steel grater has many fine teeth, while the porcelain variety has fewer and more coarse teeth.

Hand Food Mill—A stainless-steel hand food mill can come in handy when puréeing tofu and other foods for salad dressings. It has many uses in macrobiotic cooking.

Japanese Box Grater—This small, rectangular box with interchangable blades permits both simple and fancy styles of grating. Vegetables run across the blade and slices fall into the box below. Useful when preparing a large quantity of vegetables for parties or special occasions.

Melon Baller—This utensil is helpful when scooping melon balls for use in fruit salads and kantens.

Oil Skimmer—A fine, wire-mesh strainer which is useful for removing and draining croutons, tofu, tempeh, or other foods that have been deep-fried in oil.

Paring Knife—A paring knife is useful for peeling or paring vegetables and fruits, especially for persons unaccustomed to handling a Japanese vegetable knife. Knives with quality carbon-steel blades are preferred.

Pickle Press—These plastic containers come with an adjustable pressure plate that can be screwed down to apply pressure. They are used in making pressed salads or quick pickles. A medium-sized press is sufficient for most uses.

Pressure Cooker—A variety of stainless-steel pressure cookers are available in small, medium, and large sizes. A small or medium-sized pressure cooker is suitable for most uses. A pressure cooker maintains steady cooking energy and can be used for the daily preparation of brown rice, and occasionally with other foods.

Serrated Vegetable Knife—These special knives come with serrated edges. They are used to cut vegetables in fancier styles for special occasions. Vegetables or fruits cut with these knives have a ribbed surface.

Sharpening Stone—The two basic styles of sharpening stones include a wet stone that uses water, and an oil stone. The flat, rectangular stones are best for sharpening Japanese vegetable knives.

Steamer Baskets—These come in two varieties: a collapsible stainless-steel basket that fits inside the pot, and a tiered bamboo basket that fits on top of the pot. Either variety can be used for steaming.

Strainers—Strainers are used for rinsing grains, beans, pasta, seeds, and other foods. Both fine- and wider-mesh strainers are useful. Colanders, which are also used for washing and rinsing foods, are also useful.

Suribachi—These earthenware grinding bowls are made with grooved interiors. They are essential for hand grinding condiments and other foods. They come with a wooden pestle called a surikogi. A medium-sized suribachi is sufficient for most uses.

Tamari Dispenser—These small glass bottles contain spouts for pouring tamari soy sauce, oil, or natural vinegar. A useful item in the kitchen.

Vegetable Brushes—These small natural-bristle brushes are essential for cleaning vegetables and fruits. They can also be used for cleaning utensils. Two brushes—one for vegetables and the other for utensils—are very useful.

Vegetable Knife—Quality vegetable knives from Japan are designed especially for smooth and elegant cutting. They are available in stainless-steel, carbon-steel, or high-grade carbon-steel models, all with comfortable wooden handles. They

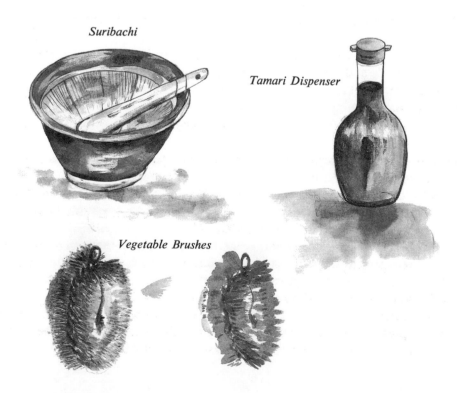

Suribachi

Tamari Dispenser

Vegetable Brushes

Vegetable Knife

Rice Paddle

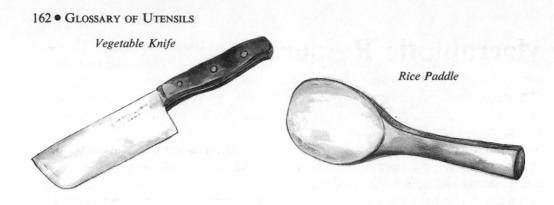

come with rectangular, rounded, or pointed tipped blades. The basic rectangular style is sufficient for most cutting styles.

Vegetable Peeler—This utensil can be used on occasion to remove waxed skins from cucumbers or other fruits or vegetables, and to make fancier cuts.

Wooden Utensils—Wood does not scratch the surface of pots and pans and does not leave a metallic taste in foods. Wooden utensils—including spoons, salad and pasta forks, chopsticks, and rice paddles—are elegant and easy to use. Hardwood utensils last many years if properly cared for.

Macrobiotic Resources

Macrobiotic Way of Life Seminar

The Macrobiotic Way of Life Seminar is an introductory program offered by the Kushi Institute in Boston. It includes classes in macrobiotic cooking, home care, kitchen setup, lectures on the philosophy of macrobiotics and the standard diet, and individual way of life guidance. It is presented monthly and includes introductory and intermediate level programs. Information on the Way of Life Seminar is available from:

> The Kushi Institute
> 17 Station Street
> Brookline, Massachusetts 02146
> (617) 738–0045

Macrobiotic Residential Seminar

The Macrotiotic Residential Seminar is an introductory program offered at the Kushi Foundation Berkshires Center in Becket, Massachusetts. It is a one week live-in program that includes hands-on training in macrobiotic cooking and home care, lectures on the philosophy and practice of macrobiotics, and meals prepared by a specially trained cooking staff. It is presented monthly and includes introductory and intermediate levels. Information on the Macrobiotic Residential Seminar is available from:

> Kushi Foundation Berkshires Center
> Box 7
> Becket, Massachusetts 01223
> (413) 623–5742

Kushi Institute Leadership Studies

For those who wish to study further, the Kushi Institute offers instruction for individuals who wish to become trained and certified macrobiotic teachers. Leadership training programs are also offered at Kushi Institute affiliates in London, Amsterdam, Antwerp, Florence, as well as in Portugal and Switzerland. Information on Leadership Studies is available from the Kushi Institute in Boston, Massachusetts.

Other Programs

The Kushi Institute offers a variety of public programs including an annual Summer Conference in western Massachusetts, special weight-loss and natural beauty seminars, and intensive cooking and spiritual development training at the Berkshires Center. Moreover, a variety of introductory and public programs are offered through an international network of over 300 educational centers in the United States, Canada, and throughout the world. The Kushi Foundation publishes a *Worldwide Macrobiotic Directory* every year listing these centers and individuals. Please consult the *Directory* for the nearest macrobiotic center or qualified instructor.

Publications

Michio and Aveline Kushi have authored numerous books on macrobiotic cooking, philosophy, diet, and way of life. These titles are listed in the Recommended Reading list and are available at macrobiotic centers, natural food stores, and bookstores. Ongoing developments are reported in *Return to Paradise*, a quarterly magazine available by subscription from the Kushi Foundation Berkshires Center.

Recommended Reading

Books

Aihara, Cornellia: *The Dō of Cooking*. Chico, Calif.: George Ohsawa Macrobiotic Foundation, 1972.

——. *Macrobiotic Childcare*. Oroville, Calif.: George Ohsawa Macrobiotic Foundation, 1971.

——. *Macrobiotic Kitchen: Key to Good Health*. Tokyo & New York: Japan Publications, Inc., 1982.

Aihara, Herman. *Basic Macrobiotics*. Tokyo & New York: Japan Publications, Inc., 1985.

Benedict, Dirk. *Confessions of a Kamikaze Cowboy*. Van Nuys, Calif.: Newcastle, 1987.

Brown, Virginia, with Susan Stayman. *Macrobiotic Miracle: How a Vermont Family Overcame Cancer*. Tokyo & New York: Japan Publications, Inc., 1985.

Dietary Goals for the United States. Washington, D. C.: Select Committee on Nutrition and Human Needs, U.S. Senate, 1977.

Diet, Nutrition, and Cancer. Washington, D. C.: National Academy of Sciences, 1982.

Dufty, William. *Sugar Blues*. New York: Warner Books, 1975.

Esko, Wendy. *Aveline Kushi's Introducing Macrobiotic Cooking*. Tokyo & New York: Japan Publications, Inc., 1987.

Esko, Edward and Wendy. *Macrobiotic Cooking for Everyone*. Tokyo & New York: Japan Publications, Inc., 1980.

Esko, Edward, ed. *Doctors Look at Macrobiotics*. Tokyo & New York: Japan Publications, Inc., 1988.

Fukuoka, Masanobu. *The Natural Way of Farming*. Tokyo & New York: Japan Publications, Inc., 1985.

——. *The Road Back to Nature*. Tokyo & New York: Japan Publications, Inc., 1987.

——. *The One-Straw Revolution*. Emmaus, Pa.: Rodale Press, 1978.

Healthy People: The Surgeon General's Report on Health Promotion and Disease Prevention, Washington, D. C.: Government Printing Office, 1979.

Heidenry, Carolyn. *Making the Transition to a Macrobiotic Diet*. Wayne, N. J.: Avery Publishing Group, 1987.

Hippocrates. *Hippocratic Writings*. Edited by G. E. R. Lloyd. Translated by J. Chadwick and W. N. Mann. New York: Penguin Books, 1978.

I Ching or Book of Changes. Translated by Richard Wilhelm and Cary F. Baynes. Princeton: Bollingen Foundation, 1950.

Ineson, John. *The Way of Life: Macrobiotics and the Spirit of Christianity*. Tokyo & New York: Japan Publications, Inc., 1986.

Ishida, Eiwan. *Genmai: Brown Rice for Better Health*. Tokyo & New York: Japan Publications, Inc., 1988.

Jack, Gale with Alex Jack. *Promenade Home: Macrobiotics and Women's Health*. Tokyo & New York: Japan Publications, Inc., 1988.

Jacobs, Barbara and Leonard. *Cooking with Seitan: The Delicious Natural Food from Whole Grain*. Tokyo & New York: Japan Publications, Inc., 1986.

Jacobson, Michael. *The Changing American Diet*. Washington, D. C.: Center for Science in the Public Interest, 1978.

Kaibara, Ekiken. *Yojokun: Japanese Secrets of Good Health*. Tokyo: Tokuma Shoten, 1974.

Kidder, Ralph D. and Edward F. Kelly. *Choice for Survival: The Baby Boomer's Dilemma*. Tokyo & New York: Japan Publications, Inc., 1988.

Kohler, Jean and Mary Alice. *Healing Miracles from Macrobiotics*. West Nyack, N. Y.: Parker, 1979.

Kotzsch, Ronald. *Macrobiotics: Yesterday and Today*. Tokyo & New York: Japan Publications, Inc., 1985.

——. *Macrobiotics Beyond Food*. Tokyo & New York: Japan Publications, Inc., 1988.

Kushi, Aveline. *How to Cook with Miso*. Tokyo & New York: Japan Publications, Inc., 1978.

——. *Lessons of Night and Day*. Wayne, New Jersey: Avery Publishing Group, 1985.

Kushi Aveline. *Macrobiotic Food and Cooking Series: Arthritis; Stress and Hypertension*. Tokyo & New York: Japan Publications, Inc., 1988.

——. *Macrobiotic Food and Cooking Series: Diabetes and Hypoglycemia; Allergies*. Tokyo & New York: Japan Publications, Inc., 1985.

——. *Macrobiotic Food and Cooking Series: Obesity, Weight Loss, and Eating Disorders; Infertility and Reproductive Disorders*. Tokyo & New York: Japan Publications, Inc., 1987.

Kushi, Aveline, with Alex Jack. *Aveline Kushi's Complete Guide to Macrobiotic Cooking*. New York: Warner Books, 1985.

——. *Aveline: The Life and Dream of the Woman Behind Macrobiotics Today*. Tokyo & New York: Japan Publications, Inc., 1988.

Kushi, Aveline and Michio. *Macrobiotic Pregnancy and Care of the Newborn*. Edited by Edward and Wendy Esko. Tokyo & New York: Japan Publications, Inc., 1984.

——. *Macrobiotic Child Care and Family Health*. Tokyo & New York: Japan Publications, Inc., 1986.

Kushi, Aveline, and Wendy Esko. *Macrobiotic Family Favorites*. Tokyo & New York: Japan Publications, Inc., 1987.

——. *The Changing Seasons Macrobiotic Cookbook*. Wayne, N. J.: Avery Publishing Group, 1983.

——. *The Macrobiotic Cancer Prevention Cookbook*. Wayne, New Jersey: Avery Publishing Group, 1986.

——. *The Quick and Natural Macrobiotic Cookbook*. New York & Chicago: Contemporary Books, 1989.

Kushi Aveline, with Wendy Esko. *The Macrotiotic Cancer Prevention Cookbook*. Garden City Park, NY: Avery Publishing Group, 1988.

Kushi, Michio. *The Book of Dō-In: Exercise for Physical and Spiritual Development*. Tokyo & New York: Japan Publications, Inc., 1979.

——. *The Book of Macrobiotics: The Universal Way of Health, Happiness and Peace*. Tokyo & New York: Japan Publications, Inc., 1986 (Rev. ed.).

——. *Cancer and Heart Disease: The Macrobiotic Approach to Degenerative Disorders*. Tokyo & New York: Japan Publications, Inc., 1986 (Rev. ed.).

——. *Crime and Diet: The Macrobiotic Approach*. Tokyo & New York: Japan Publications, Inc., 1987.

——. *The Era of Humanity*. Brookline, Mass.: East West Journal, 1980.

——. *How to See Your Health: The Book of Oriental Diagnosis*. Tokyo & New York: Japan Publications, Inc., 1980.

——. *Macrobiotic Health Education Series: Diabetes and Hypoglycemia; Allergies*. Tokyo & New York: Japan Publications, Inc., 1985.

——. *Macrobiotic Health Education Series: Arthritis*. Tokyo & New York: Japan Publications, Inc., 1988.

——. *Macrobiotic Health Education Series: Stress and Hypertension*. Tokyo & New York: Japan Publications, Inc., 1989.

——. *Macrobiotic Health Education Series: Obesity, Weight Loss, and Eating Disorders; Infertility and Reproductive Disorders*. Tokyo & New York: Japan Publications, Inc., 1987.

——. *Natural Healing through Macrobiotics*. Tokyo & New York: Japan Publications, Inc., 1978.

——. *On the Greater View: Collected Thoughts on Macrobiotics and Humanity*. Wayne, New Jersey: Avery Publishing Group, 1985.

——. *Your Face Never Lies*. Wayne, N. J.: Avery Publishing Group, 1983.

Kushi, Michio, and Alex Jack. *The Cancer-Prevention Diet*. New York: St. Martin's Press, 1983.

——. *Diet for a Strong Heart*. New York: St. Martin's Press, 1984.

Kushi, Michio, with Alex Jack. *One Peaceful World*. New York: St. Martin's Press, 1987.

Kushi, Michio, and Associates. *Doctors Look at Macrotiotics*. Edited by Edward Esko. Tokyo & New York: Japan Publications, Inc., 1988.

Kushi, Michio and Aveline, with. Alex Jack. *The Macrobiotic Diet*. Tokyo & New York: Japan Publications, Inc., 1985.

Kushi, Michio and Martha C. Cottrell. *AIDS: Macrobiotics and Natural Immunity*. Tokyo & New York: Japan Publications, Inc., 1989.

Kushi, Michio, and the East West Foundation. *The Macrobiotic Approach to Cancer*. Wayne, N. J.: Avery Publishing Group, 1982.

Kushi, Michio, with Olivia Oredson Saunders. *Macrobiotic Palm Healing*. Tokyo & New York: Japan Publications, Inc., 1988.

Kushi, Michio, with Stephen Blauer. *The Macrobiotic Way*. Wayne, New Jersey: Avery Publishing Group, 1985.

Kushi, Michio with Olivia Oredson. *Macrobiotic Palm Healing: Energy at Your Fingertips*. Tokyo & New York: Japan Publications, Inc., 1988.

Levin, Cecile Tovah. *Cooking for Regeneration: Macrobiotic Relief from Cancer, AIDS, and Degenerative Disease*. Tokyo & New York: Japan Publications, Inc., 1988.

Mendelsohn, Robert S., M.D. *Confessions of a Medical Heretic*. Chicago: Contemporary Books, 1979.

——. *Male Practice*. Chicago: Contemporary Books, 1980.

Nussbaum, Elaine. *Recovery: From Cancer to Health through Macrobiotics*. Tokyo & New York: Japan Publications, Inc., 1986.

Nutrition and Mental Health. Washington, D. C.: Select Committee on Nutrition and Human Needs, U.S. Senate, 1977, 1980.

Ohsawa, George, *Cancer and the Philosophy of the Far East*. Oroville, Calif.: George Ohsawa Macrobiotic Foundation, 1971 edition.

——. *You Are All Sanpaku*. Edited by William Dufty, New York: University Books, 1965.

——. *Zen Macrobiotics*. Los Angeles: Ohsawa Foundation, 1965.

Ohsawa, Lima. *Macrobiotic Cuisine*. Tokyo & New York: Japan Publications, Inc., 1984.

Polatin, Betsy. *Macrobiotics in Motion: Yin and Yang in Moving Spirals*. Tokyo & New York: Japan Publications, Inc., 1987.

Price, Western, A., D.D.S. *Nutrition and Physical Degeneration*. Santa Monica, Calif.: Price-Pottenger Nutritional Foundation, 1945.

Sattilaro, Anthony, M.D., with Tom Monte. *Recalled by Life: The Story of My Recovery from Cancer*. Boston: Houghton-Mifflin, 1982.

Schauss, Alexander. *Diet, Crime, and Delinquency*. Berkeley, Calif.: Parker House, 1980.

Scott, Neil E., with Jean Farmer. *Eating with Angels*. Tokyo & New York: Japan Publications, Inc., 1986.

Sergel, David. *The Macrobiotic Way of Zen Shiatsu*. Tokyo & New York: Japan Publications, Inc., 1988.

Tara, William. *A Challenge to Medicine*. Tokyo & New York: Japan Publications, Inc., 1988.

——. *Macrobiotics and Human Behavior*. Tokyo & New York: Japan Publications, Inc., 1985.

Wood, Rebecca. *Quinoa the Supergrain: Ancient Food for Today*. Tokyo & New York: Japan Publications, Inc., 1988.

Yamamoto, Shizuko. *Barefoot Shiatsu*. Tokyo & New York: Japan Publications, Inc., 1979.

The Yellow Emperor's Classic of Internal Medicine. Translated by Ilza Veith, Berkeley: University of California Press, 1949.

About the Authors

Aveline Kushi was born in 1923 in a small mountain village in the Izumo area of Japan. At college she was a star gymnast, but her athletic career was cut short by World War II. During the war she taught elementary school in her mountain district and after the war became involved in world peace activities at the Student World Government Association near Tokyo, directed by George Ohsawa. In 1951 she came to the United States and married Michio Kushi. Along with her husband, she has devoted her life to spreading macrobiotics. As co-founder of Erewhon, the *East West Journal*, the East West Foundation, the Kushi Institute, and the Kushi Foundation, she has taken an active role in macrobiotic education and development.

During the last twenty years in the Boston area, many thousands of young people have visited and studied at her home in order to change their way of life in a more natural direction. She has given countless seminars on macrobiotic cooking, pregnancy and child care, and medicinal cooking for cancer, heart disease, and AIDS patients. She has been instrumental in arranging visits to the United States by teachers and performers of such traditional arts as the Tea Ceremony, Noh Drama, and Buddhist meditation.

Aveline has written and illustrated several books including *Aveline Kushi's Complete Guide to Macrobiotic Cooking* (Warner Books, 1985), *The Changing Seasons Macrobiotic Cookbook* (Avery Publishing Group, 1985), *Macrobiotic Diet* (Japan Publications, Inc., 1985), *Macrobiotic Child Care and Family Health* (Japan Publications, Inc., 1986), and *The Macrobiotic Cancer Prevention Cookbook* (Avery Publishing Group, 1988). The mother of five children and the grandmother of five, she resides in Brookline and Becket, Massachusetts, and with her husband, spends about half the year teaching abroad. Her autobiography, *Aveline: The Life and Dream of the Woman Behind Macrobiotics Today*, was published in 1988 by Japan Publications, Inc.

Wendy Esko was born in upstate New York in 1949. She began macrobiotic studies in Boston in 1973, and with her husband, Edward, pioneered macrobiotic educational programs in the 1970s, including summer study programs at Amherst College in Massachusetts and annual conferences on the macrobiotic approach to cancer. She has taught macrobiotic cooking for more than twelve years, and is the former director of the Kushi Institute School of Cooking in Brookline, Massachusetts. She has coauthored several popular books, including *Macrobiotic Cooking for Everyone* (Japan Publications, Inc., 1980), and with Aveline, *The Changing Seasons Macrobiotic Cookbook* (Avery Publishing Group, 1985) and *Aveline Kushi's Introducing Macrobiotic Cooking* (Japan Publications, Inc., 1987), and *The Macrobiotic Cancer Prevention Cookbook* (Avery Publishing Group, 1988). Wendy lives with her husband and seven children in western Massachusetts, and teaches at the Kushi Institute in Becket.

Index

acorn squash, 23
Acteria, 31
additives, 19
aemono, 31
aerobics, 30
agar-agar, 24, 28, 38, 39, 144
   use of in kanten, 155
Agar-agar Squares with Miso-
   Apple Dressing, 150
aging, 33
AIDS, 30
alcohol, 15
alfalfa seeds, 26, 46
alfalfa sprouts, 119
almonds, 26
amazaké, 27, 28
Amazaké-Blueberry Pudding,
   153
Amazaké-Pear or Apple
   Pudding, 154
Amazaké-Tangerine Pudding,
   153
American Cancer Society,
   10, 18
American Heart Association,
   10, 18
animal foods
   comparison of to plant
     foods, 14
   effect of on digestive
     sytem, 17
   effects of, 14
   role of in human diet, 17
   yin and yang
     classification of, 14
antibiotics, 16
Aonori, 90
apple cider, 29
apple cider vinegar, 92
apple juice, 28, 92
Apple-Pear-Raisin Kanten,
   156
apples, 25
appreciation, for food, 29
apricot juice, 28
apricots, 25
arame, 25, 144
Arame-Corn Salad, 147

arepas, 22
arthritis, 37
aspics
   bean, 38
   sea-vegetable, 38
   vegetable, 38
aspirin, 16, 23
attitude, 29
autumn cooking, 34
Autumn-Winter Fruit Salad,
   152
*Aveline Kushi's Introducing
   Macrobiotic Cooking*, 35
avocado, 15
Azuki Bean-Raisin Aspic, 141
azuki beans, 24
   cooking time for, 136
   varieties of, 14

Baifun Salad, 117
baked puffed wheat gluten, 22
baking, 32
balance
   in cooking, 31
   in diet, 10
banana, 15
bancha stem tea, 28
bancha twig tea, 28
barley, 20
   preparation of, 111
   varieties and uses of, 110
barley flour products, 20
barley grain, 20
barley malt, 27, 92
Barley Salad, 111
bean aspics, 141
beans
   cooking of, 24
   cooking methods for, 135
   cooking time for, 136
   preparation of for
     cooking, 40, 135
   soaking time for, 43
   varieties of, 24
   yin and yang
     classification of, 14
bean salads, 38, 135, 137

bean sprouts, 24, 38
Becker, Marion Rombauer, 35
beefsteak plant, 90
beer, 28
Begin endive, 119
beverages, varieties of, 28
blackberries, 25
black-eyed beans, 24
black sesame seeds, 26
black soybeans, 24
   cooking time for, 137
black turtle beans, 24, 137
blanched salads, 123
blanched vegetables, 38
blanching, 40
   instructions for, 121
bluefish, 25
body care products, 30
body scrubbing, 29
Boiled Salad, 123, 124
boiled salads, 38
boiling, 32, 40
   for beans, 136
   instructions for, 106
bok choy, 23, 119
bonito flakes, 45, 93, 117
Brazil nuts, 26
bread, 22
broccoli, 23, 120
brown rice, 20
   cooking methods for, 106
   preparation of, 106
   variety of, 105
   yin and yang
     classification of, 14
   yin and yang qualities of,
     11
brown rice cream, 20
brown rice flakes, 20
Brown Rice Pudding, 154
Brown Rice Salad, 107
brown rice sushi, 109
brown rice vinegar, 27, 39, 92
buckwheat, 22
   preparation of, 114
   variety of, 114
buckwheat flour products, 22
buckwheat groats, 22

buckwheat noodles, 22, 115
buckwheat pastas, 22
Buckwheat Salad, 114
bulgur, 22, 113
Bulgur Salad, 113
burdock root, 23
    yin and yang qualities of, 11
Burdock with Sesame Dressing, 123
buttercup squash, 23
butternut squash, 23

cabbage, 23
    yin and yang qualities of, 11
Cabbage and Carrot Aspic, 130
cancer, 17, 18, 38
    and diet, 17
cantaloupe, 25, 77
carp, 25
Carrot Curls, 52, 53
Carrot Flowers, 54, 55
carrot juice, 29
Carrot Maple Leaves, 56, 57
carrots, 23
    yin and yang qualities of, 11
Carrot-top and Sesame Condiment, 91
carrot tops, 23, 120
cashews, 26
cauliflower, 23
celery, 23
Celery Curls, 65
celery juice, 29
celery leaves, 120
celery mustard, 119
celery root, 23
cellulose, 32, 36
cereal-grain coffee, 28
cereal grains, 20
    yin and yang classification of, 14
Changing Seasons Macrobiotic Cookbook, 35
charcoal broiling, 37
chemical fertilizers, 19
cherrystone clams, 25
chestnuts, 26
chewing, 30
chick-peas, 24

cooking time for, 136
Chick-pea-Vegetable Salad, 137
chicory, 119
Chinese cabbage, 23, 119
chives, 23, 92
chlorophyll, 14
chocolate, 15
cholesterol, 9, 17
chopped nuts, 45, 47
chopped scallions, 28
chopped seeds, 47
citrus, 15
    use of, 151
clean leaves, 45
Clear Aspic, 129
climate
    adaptation to, 33
    dietary adjustments for, 19
    influence of on diet, 19
cocaine, 16
coconuts, 37
cod, 25
coffee, 15, 28
collard greens, 23
collards, 120
colon cancer, 17
colorings, 19
commercial dressings, 92
commercial tea, 28
complex carbohydrates, 9, 15, 18, 19
compotes, 153
condiments, 39, 88
    use of on salads, 39, 88
    varieties of, 27
constipation, 17
cooked miso with scallions or onions, 27
cooked nori condiment, 27
cooked, thinly sliced shiitake mushrooms, 45
cooking
    effects of on food, 31
    methods of, 32
    origin of, 36
    preparation for, 40
    principles of, 31
cooking methods
    used in making salads, 40
    for vegetables, 23
cooking styles, 33
cooking times, 32

cooking utensils, 29
corn, 22
corn flour products, 22
corn grits, 22
cornmeal, 22
corn on the cob, 22
corn seeds, 27
cosmetics, 28
couscous, 22, 113
Couscous Salad, 113
crab, 25
cracked grains, 22
cracked wheat, 113
crackers, 22
cravings, cause of, 18
Creamy Tofu Dressing, 128
cress, 119
croutons, 39, 45, 46
crudités, 39, 103
Crudités, 124
cucumber, 23
Cucumber Baskets, 66
Cucumber Boat, 70, 71
Cucumber Funs, 60, 61
Cucumber Salad, 128
Cucumber Twists, 62, 63
custards, 153
cutting methods, 49

Daikon-Cucumber-Lemon Dressing, 103
Daikon Curls, 64, 65
daikon greens, 119
Daikon-Lemon Pickles, 133
daikon radish, 23
    use of as garnish, 45
daikon radish seeds, 46
Daikon-Sauerkraut Pickles, 133
dairy food, yin and yang classification of, 14
dandelion, 119
dandelion greens, 23
dandelion root, 23
dandelion tea, 28
dashi, 92
deep-fried tempeh cubes, 111
deep-frying, 37, 40, 47
degenerative diseases, 17
desserts, 39
    varieties of, 28
diabetes, 38
    and diet, 18

diet
    and cancer, 17
    and diabetes, 18
    and health, 17
    and heart disease 17
    optimum proportion of
        16
dietary awareness 9
dietary guidelines 10
digestive system, 36
    effect of food on, 17
diluting, 43
dips, 103
Discourse of Slallets, 31, 38
drawing motion, 50
dressings, 39, 88
    instructions for adding,
        93
dried chestnuts, soaking
    time for, 43
dried daikon, soaking time
    for, 43
dried fish, 25
dried foods, preparation of
    for cooking, 42
Dried Fruit Compote, 155
Dried Fruit Kanten, 157
dried fruits, soaking time
    for, 43
dried lotus root, soaking time
    for, 43
dried tofu, 24
    soaking time for, 43
dry-roasting, 32, 46
dulse, 24, 90, 144
Dulse-Cucumber Salad, 148
Dulse-Lettuce Salad, 148
Dulse Salad, 147

eggplant, 15
electricity, use in home, 30
electric stoves, 30
endive, 23, 119
energy of food, 12
enzymes, 9
escarole, 23, 119
Eskimo, 20
Evelyn, John, 31
exercise, 29

fabrics, 29
fancy vegetable and fruit

garnishes, 45
fat, 19
fermentation, 33, 36
fermented soybean products,
    15
fiber, 9, 19
filberts, 26
finger food, 39
Finger Food Salad, 124
fire
    origin of in cooking, 36
    use of in cooking, 31
fish, variety of, 25
five tastes, 92
flavorings, 19
flounder, 25
flour, percentage of in
    macrobiotic diet, 22
flour products, 22
    effects of on health, 33
flowers, 45
food
    as energy, 12
    yin and yang
        classification of, 12
food cravings, 18
food irradiation, 118
food mill, 44
food processing, 33, 36
Fresh Garden Salad, 127
freshness in diet, 37
Fresh Strawberries in Sauce,
    153
fresh tofu, 24
frozen food, 37
fruit
    energy of, 151
    preparation of for
        cooking, 42, 151
    quality of, 151
    variety of, 25, 151
    yin and yang
        classification of, 15
fruit kanten, 156
fruit salad, 38, 151
fu, 22
    soaking time for, 43

garbanzo beans, 24
garnishes, 39
    fancy, 51
    use of with seafood, 25
    varieties of, 28, 45

gas range, 30
gelatin, 37–39
gelatin salads, 37
ginger, 92
ginger juice, 92
Glazed Peaches with Tofu
    Cheese Slices, 152
gomashio, 27
    definition of, 89
Gomashio, 89
grains
    preparation of for
        cooking, 40
    soaking time for, 43
grain salad, 90
grape juice, 28
grapes, 25
grated daikon, 27, 28, 44, 45,
    92
Grated Daikon with Toasted
    Nori Strips, 149
grated fruits, 48, 92
grated ginger, 27, 44, 45
grated horseradish, 28, 45
grated radish, 27, 28
grated raw daikon, 25
grated vegetables, 48
grated wasabi, 45
grating, 44
    use of in making
        garnish, 48
great northen beans, 24
green beans, 23
Green Beans with Sesame
    Seed Dressing, 139
green cabbage, 119
Green Goddess Dressing, 102
green mustard paste, 27
Green Nori Flake Condi-
    ment, 90
green nori flakes, 27, 45, 90
Green Nori Flakes, 149
Green Nori Flake-Shiso-
    Sesame Condiment, 91
green peas, 23
green peppers, 36
greens, 35
grilling, 32, 37
grinding, 43
ground vegetables
    flavors of, 120
    preparation of for
        cooking, 41
    varieties of, 120

haddock, 25
halibut, 25
harmony in cooking, 31
hato mugi, 110
hato mugi vinegar, 92
health and diet, 17
heart attack, 17
heart disease, 18
    and diet, 17
heat, effect of on food, 32
hemoglobin, 14
herbal beverages, 28
herba salata, 35, 37
herbs, 36, 93
herring, 25
high blood pressure, 18
hijiki, 24, 144
Hijiki Salad, 145
Hokkaido, 15
Hokkaido pumpkin, 23
home gardening, 118
honey, 15
honeydew melon, 25, 77
horseradish, 25, 92
hubbard squash, 23
hummus, 70
Hummus, 103

ice age, 36
immune deficiencies, 38
insulin, 18
iriko, 25
Irish moss, 24
Iceberg lettuce, 23

Japanese mountain potato, 23
Japanese noodles, 115
Japanese vegetable knife, 52
Jerusalem artichoke, 23
Jinenjo, 23
*Journal of the American
    Dental Association*, 30
Joy of Cooking, The, 35
Julienne-style Vegetable
    Bundles, 58, 59

kale, 23, 119
kanpyo, 149
kanten, 38, 39, 68, 151
    definition of, 155
kasha, 9, 22, 114

kelp, 90
Kidney Bean-Dandelion
    Salad, 138
kidney beans, 24
    cooking time for, 136
kiwi, 15
knife technique, use in
    cooking, 49
kohlrabi, 23
kohlrabi leaves, 120
kombu, 24, 90, 144, 149
    use of in cooking beans,
    24, 136
kombu broth, 92
kombu-Carrot Rolls, 141
kombu dashi, 92
kombu tea, 28
Kushi Foundation, 20

leafy greens
    flavor of, 119
    preparation of for
        cooking, 41, 119
    varieties of, 119
leeks, 23
Lemon Baskets, 36, 37
Lemon Butterflies, 38
lemon juice, 27, 92
Lemon Pudding, 144
lemon rind, 45
lemons, 45
lemon slices, 28, 45
lemon twists, 45
Lemon Twists, 72, 73
lemon wedges, 45
Lentil Aspic, 142
Lentil Pâté, 104
lentils, cooking time for, 136
lettuce, 119
    role of in modern diet, 37
lifestyle, 29
lima beans, 24
    cooking time for, 137
Lime Baskets, 66
Lime Butterflies, 68, 69
lime juice, 92
lime slices, 45
lime twists, 45
Lime Twists, 73
lime wedges, 45
littleneck clams, 25
lobster, 25
Lotus Flowers, 80, 81

lotus root, 23, 81
lotus root tea, 28
low-fat cuisine, 9

macadamia nuts, 26
macaroni, 116
macrobiotic diet, 10, 20
    salads in, 37
macrobiotic dietary
    guidelines, 19
macrobiotic education, 9
Macrobiotic Family Favorite,
    34, 88
macrobiotic lifestyle, 29
Macrobiotic Residential
    Seminar, 20
macrobiotics, definition of, 9
Macrobiotic Way of Life
    Seminar, 20, 38
maple syrup, 15
marijuana, 16
Marinated Daikon and
    Carrot Salad, 126
Marinated Lotus Root
    Salad, 126
marinated tofu, 48
marinated tofu cubes, 45
marinating, 43
    instructions for, 121
marshmallows, 37
martial arts, 30
matzos, 22
mayonnaise, 93
meal planning, 39
meals, regularity of, 30
Melon Fans, 76, 77
microwave oven, 30
millet, 22
    preparation of, 112
    variety of, 112
Millet and Chick-pea Salad,
    112
millet flour products, 22
millet grain, 22
minced vegetables, 48
mincing, 48
minerals, 9, 19
    effects of on food, 32
mirin, 27, 92
miso, 15, 27, 48, 92
Miso-Apple Dressing, 95
Miso-Brown Rice Vinegar
    Dressing, 93

Miso-Cucumber Pickles, 134
miso dressings, 93
Miso-Ginger Dressing, 94
Miso-Lemon Dressing, 94
Miso-Mirin-Vinegar
    Dressing, 96
Miso-Mustard Dressing, 94
Miso-Orange Dressing, 94
miso soup, 22
Miso-Tahini Dressing, 94
Miso-Tofu-Tahini Dressing, 96
Miso-Umeboshi Vinegar
    Dressing, 95
Miso-Ume-Tahini Dressing, 95
Miso-Walnut Dressing, 95
mixed aspics, 39
mixed kantens, 39
Mixed Pressed Salad, 125
mixed salads, 39
mizuna, 119
mochi, 20, 26
modern diet, 37
    rise of, 17
molasses, 15
Much Depends on Dinner, 37
muffins, 22
mulberries, 25
mung beans, 24, 46
mung bean sprouts, 46
Mung Bean Sprout Salad,
    128, 139
Mung Bean Thread Noodle
    Salad, 117
mushrooms, 23
mustard greens, 23, 119
    yin and yang qualities
        of, 11
Mu tea, 28

National Academy of
    Sciences, 10, 18
natto, 24
natto salads, 141
Natto with Grated Daikon,
    141
Natto with Mustard, 141
natural food movement, 9
natural vinegar, 38
navy beans, 24
    cooking time for, 137
Navy Bean Salad, 138
nightshade vegetables, 15, 37
noodles

preparation of, 115
    varieties of, 115
noodle salads, 114
nori, 24, 144
    instructions for
        toasting, 46
    use in sushi, 109
nori strips, 45
Nori-Vegetable Sushi, 148
northern beans, cooking
    time for, 147
nutrients in sea vegetables, 144
nutrition, awareness of, 9
nuts, 47
    varieties of, 26

oat flakes, 22
oat flour products, 22
oatmeal, 22
oats, 22
ohitashi, 121
oil
    effects of on food, 33
    effects of on health, 36
    use of in macrobiotic
        cooking, 33
    use as salad dressing, 35
okara, 24
olive oil, 27, 36
onion, 23
orange juice, 27, 28
orange slices, 28
organic foods, 19
organic produce, 118
oven-roasting, 44, 47
oyster, 25

pak choi, 119
pancakes, 22
pancreas, 18
paring knife, 56
parsley, 23, 28, 92, 120
Parsley and Sesame Condi-
    ment, 91
Parsley with Pumpkin-seed
    Dressing, 124
pasta, 9, 23
pasta salads, 38, 105, 114
patty pan squash, 23
peaches, 25
peanuts, 26
pearl barley, 20, 110

pearled barley, 20
pecans, 26
peppers, 15
persimmon, 25
pickles, 38, 39
    varieties of, 26
pickling, 33, 40
pineapple, 15
pine needles, 45
pine nuts, 26
pinto beans, 24
    cooking time for, 137
plant foods
    comparison of to animal
        foods, 14
    effects of, 14
    role of in human diet, 16
plants, yin and yang
    classification of, 13
plums, 25
"polar-tropical" diet, 17
popped corn, 22
poppy seeds, 26
positive attitude, 29
potassium, 14
potato, 15, 36
powdered sea-vegetable
    condiments, 45
predigestion, 32
prepared dressings, 93
pre-roasting, instructions for,
    106
Pressed Salad, 125
pressed salads, 35, 39, 121
Pressed Wakame and Lettuce
    Salad, 146
pressing, 40
    instructions for, 121
pressure-cooking, 40
    for beans, 136
    instructions for, 106
    use of in macrobiotics, 32
preventive dietary guidelines,
    10, 18
processed food, 37
protein, vegetable quality, 19
puddings, 153
puffed barley, 20
puffed brown rice, 20
puffed cereals, 26
puffed corn, 22
puffed millet, 22
pumpkin, 23
Pumpkin-seed Condiment, 91

pumpkin seeds, 26
    use as garnish, 47
Puréed Chick-pea Aspics, 142
Puréed Squash Aspic, 130
puréeing miso, 43

quick-boiling, instructions
    for, 121
quick pickles, 121, 131

radiation, 30
radish, 23
Radish Curls, 52, 53
radish greens, 119
Radish Tops, 83
raisins, 25, 45, 92
raspberries, 26
raw fruit, use of in
    macrobiotic diet, 39, 151
raw vegetables, use of in
    macrobiotic diet, 38
raw vegetable salads, 126
red cabbage, 23
red lentils, cooking time for,
    137
Red Radish Chrysanthemums,
    74
Red Radish Flowers, 84, 85
Red Radish Tops, 82, 83
red shiso leaves, 90
rice balls, 26
rice cakes, 26
rice syrup, 27, 92
roasted and chopped shiso, 27
roasted barley tea, 28
roasted brown rice tea, 28
roasted nuts, 45, 92
roasted seeds, 45, 92
roasted sesame seeds, 27
roasting, 40, 44
romain lettuce, 23
Rombauer, Irma, S., 35
root vegetables
    flavors of, 120
    preparation of in
        cooking, 41
    varieties of, 120
rumen, 36
ruminants, 36
rye, 22
rye bread, 22
rye flakes, 22

rye flour products, 22
rye grain, 22

Saifun Salad, 117
saké, 28
salad bars, 9, 31, 36, 39
salad making, 31
salads
    beans, 38
    cooking methods used
        for, 40
    definition of, 35
    effect of on digestion, 36
    effects of on health, 36
    fruit, 38
    pasta, 38
    popularity of, 9
    sea-vegetable, 38
    tofu, 38
    use of in macrobiotic
        diet, 37
    varieties of, 31
    vegetable, 38
    whole grain, 38
    yin and yang
        classification of, 36
salmon, 25
salt
    effects of on vegetables,
        35
    use of in cooking, 32
    use of in salad, 37
Salt-Brine Pickles, 132
salted greens, 35
sandwiches, 140
sardines, 25
saturated fat, 17, 19, 25
sauerkraut, 26
sautéing, 33
scallions, 23, 92
Scallion Whisks, 78, 79
scrod, 25
seafood, 9
    variety of, 25
    yin and yang
        classification of, 15
seafood salad, 70
sea palm, 144, 150
sea salt, 92
Sea Salt-Brown Rice Vinegar
    Dressing, 101
sea salt dressings, 101
seasonal changes, adaptation

to, 33
seasonal cooking, 38
seasonings, 31
    flavors of, 92
    ingredients in, 92
    use of on salads, 92
    varieties of, 27
seasons, cycles of, 12
sea-vegetable aspics, 38
sea-vegetable flakes, 92
sea-vegetable powders, 27, 89,
    92
sea vegetables
    nutritional value of, 144
    preparation of for
        cooking, 40
    soaking of, 145
    soaking time for, 43
    in traditional diets, 144
    use in condiments, 90
    varieties of, 24, 144
    washing of, 144
    yin and yang
        classification of, 15
sea-vegetable salads, 38, 144
Sea-vegetable Sprinkles, 89
seeds, 47
    preparation of for
        cooking, 40
    varieties of, 26
seitan, 22, 111
sesame butter, 92
sesame oil, 33
Sesame Salt, 89
Sesame-Sea-vegetable
    Sprinkles, 89
sesame seeds, 27, 39
    use as garnish, 47
Sesame-Shiso Condiment, 90
shellfish, 25
shiitake nushrooms, 23
    soaking time for, 43
shio kombu, 27
shiso leaf, 90
Shiso-leaf Condiments, 90
short-grain rice, 14
shredded daikon, 25
shrimp, 25
sickness, prevention of, 18
simple aspics, 39
simple kantens, 39
simple salads, 39
simple sugars, 9, 15, 18, 19
sliced chives, 45

sliced parsley, 45
sliced red-radish rounds, 45
sliced scallions, 45
Sliced Vegetable Aspic, 130
small dried fish, 25
small Spanish nuts, 26
smelt, 25
snacking, 30
snacks, 39
    varieties of, 26
snap beans, 23
snapper, 25
soaking, 22, 42
    for sea vegetables, 145
soba, 22, 45, 105, 115
Soba Salad, 116
Soba Sushi, 116
sodium, 14
soft drinks, 28
sole, 25
somen, 105, 115
Somen Salad, 115
Somen Sushi, 116
soups, varieties of, 22
Soybean Relish, 138
soybeans, 24
    cooking time for, 137
    energy quality of, 15
    nutritional qualities of, 15
soybean sprouts, 46
soy milk, 15, 28
soy sauce, 27
spices, 15, 22, 93
Split Pea Aspic, 142
split peas, 24
    cooking time for, 137
sprigs of parsley, 45
sprigs of watercress, 45
spring cooking, 34
Spring-Summer Fruit Salad, 152
spring water, 28
sprouting, 46
sprouting kits, 46
sprouts, 38, 45, 46
squash, yin and yang qualities of, 11
squash seeds, 26
Standard Macrobiotic Diet, 20, 21
steaming, 32, 40
    instructions for, 122
steel-cut oats, 22
strawberries, 26

Strawberry Kanten Pie, 156
stroke, 17
Summer Fruit Kanten, 156
summer cooking, 34
summer squash, 23
Sunflower-seed Condiment, 91
sunflower seeds, 26, 27, 39
    use as garnish, 47
sunomono, 31, 35
suribachi, 44, 89
    use of, 43
surikogi, 89
sushi, 23, 27, 90, 116
Sushi, instructions for preparing, 109
sweet brown rice, 20
sweet brown rice grain, 20
sweet brown rice products, 20
sweet brown rice vinegar, 92
sweeteners, yin and yang classification of, 15
Sweet Sea Palm Salad, 150
sweet vegetables, 92
swordfish, 25

tahini, 92
Tahini Custard, 155
tamari soy sauce, 27, 92
Tamari Soy Sauce-Bonito Flake Dressing, 98
Tamari Soy Sauce-Dashi Dressing, 98
tamari soy sauce dressings, 96
Tamari Soy Sauce-Ginger Dressing, 97
Tamari Soy Sauce-Lemon Dressing, 97
tamari soy sauce marinade, 96
Tamari Soy Sauce-Mirin Dressing, 98
Tamari Soy Sauce-Mustard Dressing, 97
Tamari Soy Sauce, Oil, and Vinegar Dressing, 98
Tamari Soy Sauce-Onion Pickles, 132
Tamari Soy Sauce-Orange Dressing, 97
Tamari Soy Sauce-Rutabaga Pickles, 131
Tamari Soy Sauce-Scallion Dressing, 97

Tamari Soy Sauce-Sesame Dressing, 98
Tamari Soy Sauce-Umeboshi Vinegar Dressing, 98
Tangerine Baskets, 66
Tangerine Butterflies, 68
tangerine juice, 27, 92
tangerine rind, 45
tangerines, 46
tangerine slices, 28, 45
tangerine twists, 45
Tangerine Twists, 73
tangerine wedges, 45
tekka, 27
tempeh, 24
Tempeh Salad, 140
tempeh salads, 139
Three Bean Salad, 137
Time, 9
time, influence of in cooking, 32
toasted nori, 45
toasted nori squares, 45
toasted nori strips, 45
tofu, 15, 48, 101
tofu cheese, 48, 70, 152
tofu-cheese cubes, 45
Tofu-cheese Dressing, 102
tofu dip, 70
Tofu Dips, 103
tofu dressings, 101
Tofu Mayonnaise, 102
Tofu-Miso Dressing, 102
Tofu Salad, 139
tofu salads, 38, 135
Tofu-Umeboshi Dressing, 102
Tofu-Vegetable Salad, 140
tomato, 15, 36
tooth structure and diet, 16
Tossed Salad, 127
traditional diets, 17
traditional foods, 19
tropical foods, 36
tropical fruit, 15, 25
    use of, 151
    use of in salads, 39
tropical vegetables, 23
trout, 25
turnip, 23
Turnip Chrysanthemums, 74, 75
Turnip Curls, 65
turnip greens, 23, 119
Turnip-Kombu Pickles, 133

udon, 105, 115
Udon Salad, 115
Udon Sushi, 116
Umeboshi-Bonito Flake
    Dressing, 101
Umeboshi-Brown Rice
    Vinegar Dressing, 100
Umeboshi-Daikon Dressing,
    100
umeboshi dressings, 89
Umeboshi-Lemon or Orange
    Dressing, 100
umeboshi-parsley dressing, 111
Umeboshi-Parsley Dressing, 99
umeboshi paste, 27, 39, 92
Umeboshi Pickles, 133
umeboshi plums, 27, 39, 92
umeboshi plum seeds, 26
Umeboshi-Scallion
    Dressing, 99
Umeboshi-Sesame Seed
    Dressing, 99
Umeboshi-Tahini Dressing,
    100
umeboshi vinegar, 27, 92
Umeboshi Vinegar-Miso
    Dressing, 100
uncooked salads, 40
U.S. Senate Select Committee
    on Nutrition and Human
    Needs, 10
universe, order of, 36
unrefined sea salt, 27
unsaturated fat, 19

variety, in cooking methods,
    33
vegetable aspics, 38, 129
Vegetable Bundles, 58
vegetable cooking, 23
Vegetable Curls, 52
vegetable cutting, 49
vegetable juices, 29
vegetables

cooking methods for, 120
cutting methods for, 50
freshness of, 118
preparation of for
    cooking, 41, 120
quality of, 118
varieties of, 23, 118
yin and yang classifica-
    tion of, 15
vegetable salads, 38, 118
Vegetable Twists, 86, 87
vegetarians, 9
vinegar
    commercial, 36
    traditional, 36
    use as salad dressing, 35
    use of in salads, 35
Visser, Margaret, 37
vitamins, 9, 19

wakame, 24, 90, 144
Wakame-Cucumber Salad, 146
Wakame-Daikon-Carrot
    Salad, 147
Wakame with Tofu Dressing,
    146
Waldorf Salad, 128
walnuts, 26
wasabi, 25, 92
washing beans, 40
washing dried foods, 42
washing fruits, 42
washing grains, 40
washing ground vegetables, 41
washing leafy vegetables, 41
washing root vegetables, 41
washing sea vegetables, 40
washing seeds, 40
water
    use of, 44
    use of in cooking, 31
watercress, 23, 92, 119
Watercress Salad with Creamy
    Tofu Dressing, 128

watermelon, 26
wax beans, 23
well water, 28
wheat
    preparation of, 113
    variety of, 113
wheat gluten, 22
wheat pastas, 115
wheat spaghetti, 115
whipped cream, 37
white-meat fish, 25
White Miso-Sesame Seed
    Dressing, 95
white sesame seeds, 26
whole dried peas, 24
whole foods, 19
whole grain salads, 38, 105
whole lettuce leaves, 45
whole oats, 22
whole wheat, 22
whole wheat berries, 22
whole wheat bread, 22
whole wheat chapatis, 22
whole wheat flakes, 22
whole wheat flour, 22
whole wheat flour products, 22
Whole Wheat Macaroni
    Salad, 116
whole wheat noodles, 22
whole wheat pastas, 22
whole wheat spaghetti, 105
wild berries, 26
wild plants, 120

yams, 15
yellow mustard paste, 27
yellow soybeans, 46
yin and yang
    in colors, 13
    definition of, 10
    in food, 10
yoga, 20
yuba, 24